9.95

Teaching and Understanding Contemporary Piano Music

Teaching
and Understanding
Contemporary Piano Music

Ellen Thompson

Kjos West

Neil A. Kjos Jr., Publisher

4382 Jutland Drive

San Diego, California 92117

Published by Kjos West

Distributed by Neil A. Kjos Music Company
4382 Jutland Drive, San Diego, California 92117

© 1976 Kjos West, San Diego, California

International Standard Book Number 0-910842-06-X

Library of Congress Card Number 76-24574

Printed and Bound in the United States of America

Edition Number WP30

To my teachers,
"Doc" Monroe, Charles Finney, Alton Cronk,
Stella Roberts and Lillian Powers–Wadsworth;
but especially to
Mother, who first taught me the "lines and spaces,"
and Dad, who "played me to sleep" each night when I was a child.

Contents

Preface

The author's yearly encounter with piano students whose literature background reveals an alarming paucity of contemporary music has prompted the writing of this book. This is an observation rather than an indictment upon the quality of their pre-college piano instruction, for the problem is not a simple one. A half-hour weekly lesson during these formative years is hardly enough to plumb the depths of the enormous volume of good literature as well as to deal with the technical development, and the aural, analytical, written and sightreading skills of the student. The fact that a great majority of private piano teachers have had only scant theory backgrounds especially in the areas of chromatic and modern harmony, including dissonant counterpoint, has further compounded the situation. Most undergraduate programs, until recently, did not contain or require courses in twentieth century music. As a consequence, many of those teachers who have not had or taken the opportunity for training in this area formally, through local workshops or by the "self-taught" method, seldom teach contemporary piano music, either out of fear of the unknown or a dislike for the unfamiliar, which to some, sounds chaotic and discordant.

Because of the diversity of technics used by twentieth century composers and the continuing evolution and experimentation that characterizes our age, theorists have ostensibly found it impractical or impossible, as yet, to offer a distillation in the form of a compact systematic theory textbook, and perhaps never will. However, several excellent books dealing with the technics used in contemporary music have been written, including Dallin's *Techniques of Twentieth Century Composition*, Marquis' *Twentieth Century Music Idioms* (contrapuntal approach; also contains a helpful bibliography), Persichetti's *Twentieth-Century Harmony*, Ulehla's *Contemporary Harmony* and the more specialized *Serial Composition and Atonality* by George Perle. Each is unique in its approach.

But for the non-professional, the high school student or the average studio piano teacher these college-level textbooks are too advanced, too technical and in some cases impractical because they contain musical examples and excerpts more complex than the literature with which these people are dealing or can cope. This book is offered as an effort to bridge this gap, for it is worth noting that most of the technics used by contemporary composers (exclusive of the avant-garde) are found in piano music, and not infrequently by well-known composers, such as Serge Prokofiev, Bela Bartok, Dmitri Kabalevsky, Paul Creston, William Schuman, Vincent Persichetti, Ernst Krenek and Igor Stravinsky, to name a few.

As we master the technical terminology for labeling the devices found in contemporary music and recognize their expressive power in the music we are playing or teaching, an understanding and appreciation will accrue which will lead to stylistic and convincing performances; interpretations based upon *both* intuition and intellect, an educated ear *and* a trained mind. Thus, *music* will be learned, not just notes. Sensitive, knowledgeable and discerning musicians will be the product, not just piano players. What teacher has not exulted over a student's expression of delight when something new has been learned. Not long ago it was my pleasure to coach a young violinist by accompanying her on the slow movement of Rode's *Concerto No. 7*. Experiencing some technical difficulty in one measure we went back to that spot for a little drill. "Oh, that's my favorite measure—I love the sound," she said. When she understood it to be the colorful and expressive Neapolitan sixth chord, which took less than thirty seconds to explain, her increased comprehension resulted not only in teenage-type excitement but also in approaching the passage *musically* which helped to remove the obstacle. She was not too young to discover that an artistic performance is contingent upon the understanding of the meaning conveyed by notational symbols whether this is intuitive or consciously learned.

Hence, this book is directed primarily to piano teachers of pre-college pupils as well as to high school and college students, and non-professionals with the hope that it will whet their appetites for greater in-depth exposure to *all* contemporary music through performance, analysis and listening. For, as Stravinsky writes in his *Autobiography*, "In music, more than in any other branch of art, understanding is given only to those who make an active effort."[1] Furthermore, our musical tastes and attitudes are largely shaped by our experience in music. Therefore, the full thrust and intent of this book will only be realized by the reader as he does, in fact, "make an active effort" by indulging in the additional resource reading, listening, playing and creative writing suggested in the assignments at the close of each chapter.

This survey of twentieth century technics cannot be entirely comprehensive because all devices do not accommodate themselves to pre-college-level piano music. It is, therefore, incumbent upon the users of this book to consider it merely as an *introduction* to twentieth century compositional technics, not as a terminal course.

---

[1] Igor Stravinsky, *An Autobiography*, p. 152.

It cannot be over-emphasized, as William Austin writes in his Preface to *Music in the 20th Century:*

> Intelligent study of any music . . . balances the accumulation of facts and interpretations with continuous practice in making music, and continuous, repeated, attentive, discriminating listening. Because of this, (those) who look for a book to help them understand 20th century music look in vain. A book cannot possibly provide the desirable balance. A book can save time if we use it to guide our practical study and listening . . . Real interest, like thirst or hunger, means seeking out the music, in notation or recorded performance or both, so as to return to it over a period of years, to discriminate with delicacy among different performances, to accumulate a repertory of an important and congenial composer's main works in various forms and media, and to relate each new experience to a gradually growing and deepening sense of the work as a whole.[2]

The writing of this book has been made possible by a Faculty Research Grant from the Wheaton College Alumni Association, to whom I owe a debt of gratitude. Much of the writer's time during that year's leave-of-absence was spent in the picturesque, rural community of Pentwater, Michigan, which not only provided a grass-roots perspective, but also opportunity to consult both a local piano teacher and high school student as to the clarity of style and the accessibility of the piano literature selected for study.

The worth and effectiveness of this book will be proven only by a perceptible increase in appreciation, as well as intelligent and artistic performances of contemporary music on the part of the readers, hopefully, teachers of future freshmen music majors.

Ellen Thompson
Wheaton, Illinois

---

[2]William W. Austin, *Music in the 20th Century*, pp. xi-xii.

Introduction

Optimum benefit from the material in this book can only be achieved by the reader as he saturates himself with the *sound* of contemporary music. No amount of reading about the music and its composers can take the place of listening to it or better still, playing it. Therefore, *playing* must always accompany the analysis of a piece in order to be sure that the ear is being trained along with the mind and fingers. Also, music, recordings and live concerts are worthwhile investments, and their contribution to the development of musical taste, perspective and growth should not be overlooked. It is recommended, then, that one purchase and play as much of the music listed in Appendix E (page 213) as possible, for most of it is pre-college-level and therefore not too difficult. In the process of studying a new work it is helpful to diagram or analyze its components. Such an understanding of its structure and content will make for easier and more accurate reading and memorization, as well as result in an authoritative and stylistic grasp of its meaning.

The writer assumes a knowledge of the vocabulary and concepts of basic harmony, melody, rhythm, counterpoint and form on the part of the reader, as most contemporary procedures are an outgrowth of their predecessors. Where there is such a derivation, comparisons will be drawn as a means of fostering a panoramic view of the historical evolution of compositional style. "The Tonal Period and Its Gradual Breakdown" is the subject of Appendix B (page 193) and should be read before embarking upon the rest of the book. (Joseph Machlis gives a thorough treatment of this subject in the opening section of his book, *Introduction to Contemporary Music*.)

One observes that twentieth century composers do not discard all the constituents of the preceding period for, as Leon Dallin says in his text, *Techniques of Twentieth Century Composition*, ". . . contemporary techniques represent additions to and expansions of previous practices and not replacements for them."[3] In light of this statement, it is not uncommon to find a rather heterogeneous vocabulary employed in contemporary music, even within the confines of a given work. This is why one cannot speak of "the" contemporary style. But we can learn about the many devices that composers use today in order to gain a greater understanding of their music.

Biographical data will also serve to increase our level of insight and is easily obtained from the many excellent books dealing with contemporary composers and their works. *The World of Twentieth Century Music* by David Ewen is particularly commendable. Also valuable are the autobiographical materials or writings of contemporary composers, such as those by Stravinsky, Hindemith and Sessions. For an exhaustive listing of pertinent publications, see William Austin's book, *Music in the 20th Century*. Statistics of this kind, of course, will eventually become obsolete or incomplete, but one can keep abreast of new releases through magazines, such as *Clavier* and *Piano Quarterly*.

It may be helpful at this point to define the term *twentieth century* or *contemporary* music, for not all music written in the 1900's can be described in this way. The date of a composition is of less significance than its style. For example, despite the fact that Debussy was born in 1862 and Brahms died in 1897, making them contemporaries for thirty-five years, their music sounds very different even to the casual listener. This is due to Debussy's interest in breaking away from such traditional tyrannies as the barline, regulator of metric accent, and tonality; whereas, Brahms adhered quite closely to these and other elements that are contained in the music of the so-called "common practice" period, a three-hundred-year span extending roughly from 1600 to 1900 (see Appendix B).

Reading contemporary music will be either a discouraging or disastrous experience if it is not accompanied or preceded by an academic knowledge of its theoretical content and rigorous drills for the hand. Mastery of scales, broken

---

[3] Leon Dallin, *Techniques of Twentieth Century Composition*, Second Edition, p. 14

chords and arpeggios as well as the technical problems contained in Cramer, Czerny and Clementi studies, which equipped the pianist to play the familiar-sounding music of previous centuries, is found to be inadequate preparation for the demands of contemporary music. The fingers must adjust to new shapes and combinations of notes, such as clusters, quartal, modal or synthetic scale patterns, while the mind and eye must learn to grasp widely-spaced groups of notes, intricate rhythms, changing meters, a maze of accidentals, etc. Samuel Adler's forty studies, called *Gradus I* and *Gradus II*, have been written for just this purpose. Notes in the front describe the compositional devices used in each of these miniature pieces.

A commendatory word is in order here about Bartok's monumental pedagogical contribution to piano literature, the six-volume *Mikrokosmos*. It has become, for many, an indispensable tool in teaching contemporary technics to the beginner before he becomes entrenched in traditional thought and finger patterns. And it is equally superb as sight reading material for the advanced player who may have already, though unwittingly, become conditioned by the familiar provincialism of tonality which can produce mental laziness in the reading process. Reference will be made to pieces in these books, but the serious student of pedagogy and contemporary literature will want to explore them in detail.

And finally, the author recommends the following small but excellent collections of contemporary piano music on the preparatory level. The *Contempo* series, *Mosaics, Adventures in Modes and Keys*, and *Adventures in Time and Space* are designed to teach twentieth century technics, so all the devices are explained or labeled. Hence, the individual pieces rarely appear in the graded lists in this book.

ELEMENTARY

    Contempo 1, edited by Mary Elizabeth Clark, Myklas Press.
    Contempo 2, edited by Mary Elizabeth Clark, Myklas Press.
    Contempos in Crimson, edited by Mary Elizabeth Clark, Myklas Press.
    Contempos in Jade, edited by Mary Elizabeth Clark, Myklas Press.
    Contempos in Orchid, edited by Mary Elizabeth Clark, Myklas Press.
    Contempos in Sapphire, edited by Mary Elizabeth Clark, Myklas Press.
    Mack, Glenn   *Adventures in Modes and Keys*, Summy-Birchard Co.

ELEMENTARY-INTERMEDIATE

Adventures in Time and Space, Vol. I (Studies for Contemporary Music), Schmitt, Hall and McCreary Co.

Adventures in Time and Space, Vol. II (Studies for Contemporary Music), Schmitt, Hall and McCreary Co.

Adventures in Time and Space, Vol. III (Studies for Contemporary Music), Schmitt, Hall and McCreary Co.

Adventures in Time and Space, Vol. IV (Studies for Contemporary Music), Schmitt, Hall and McCreary Co.

Adventures in Time and Space, Vol. V (Studies for Contemporary Music), Schmitt, Hall and McCreary Co.

Contemporary Collection, Revised Edition, Summy-Birchard Co.

Noona, Walter, and Noona, Carol *The Contemporary Performer, Book 2* (Mainstreams Piano Method), Heritage Music Press.

Noona, Walter, and Noona, Carol *The Contemporary Performer, Book 3* (Mainstreams Piano Method), Heritage Music Press.

ELEMENTARY-ADVANCED

Contemporary Piano Literature, Book 1 (Frances Clark Library), Summy-Birchard Co.

Contemporary Piano Literature, Book 2 (Frances Clark Library), Summy-Birchard Co.

Contemporary Piano Literature, Book 3 (Frances Clark Library), Summy-Birchard Co.

Contemporary Piano Literature, Book 4 (Frances Clark Library), Summy-Birchard Co.

Contemporary Piano Literature, Book 5-6 (Frances Clark Library), Summy-Birchard Co.

INTERMEDIATE

American Composers of Today, Edward B. Marks Music Corp.

Contemporary Piano Repertoire, Level 5, edited by Maurice Hinson and David Glover, Belwin-Mills Publishing Corp.

Contemporary Piano Repertoire, Level 6, edited by Maurice Hinson and David Glover, Belwin-Mills Publishing Corp.

Mosaics (32 piano pieces for learning musicianship), Sonos Music Resources, Inc.

The World of Modern Piano Music, edited by Denes Agay, MCA Music.

Chapter 1
Melody

Introduction

The typical melody of the classic-romantic tradition is often described as *vocal* whether it is in a piano piece, a symphony or song. This is due to the fact that most of these melodies possess certain features that make them singable, not least of all, the vocal range which many of them encompass. Symmetry and repetition make them easy to remember. Resolving tendency tones fulfill the expectation of the listener and produce stepwise motion much of the time. Leaps are often within one chord and are carefully chosen to give variety, to increase activity, or to emphasize points of tension and climax. In the case of large leaps, the direction changes afterwards. Cadences punctuate the melody at regular intervals allowing for breathing places every two, four or eight measures depending on the tempo; they also serve to establish or reaffirm the prevailing tonality. This strong feeling of key based upon a major or minor scale is, perhaps, the largest factor by which the listener is able to grasp the melody as a whole, as a complete idea or unit, thereby giving it meaning.

Against this backdrop, today's melodies appear more often as a series of unrelated notes than as coherent musical ideas. They defy a simple definition or description for there is no general pattern to which they must subscribe. However, a careful examination of twentieth century melodies does reveal that they are not incoherent, aimless or void of orderliness. Their initial strangeness is due to a variety of new procedures in the areas of scale basis, tonality, counterpoint, rhythm and meter.

This chapter will explore scale resources and pitch characteristics. Rhythmic features, contrapuntal treatment, formal construction and tonal aspects are dealt with in later chapters.

Scale Resources

The abandonment of the major and minor scales (and their chromatic inflections) as the exclusive resource for melody began taking place during the nineteenth century when composers such as Chopin, Franck, Dvorak, Brahms and Mussorgsky recalled the ancient church modes. (All music was associated with the church at this time; hence the name *church* or *ecclesiastical* modes.) Inherited from the Greeks of the pre-Christian era, these scales (Dorian, Phrygian, Lydian, Mixolydian) became well-established by the ninth century and were the basis for existing church music forms—the *plainsong* and *chant*. (The Locrian mode, B to B, was discarded from the beginning because the unstable diminished fifth in the tonic chord robbed it of the necessary quality of rest.) By the sixteenth century the Aeolian and Ionian modes were well-formulated. However, by the seventeenth century these six church modes had lost their individual identities due to the free use of accidentals to correct certain "wrong" notes (called *musica ficta*) reducing their number to only two, Ionian and Aeolian. These eventually became known as *major* and *minor*.

The old modes might have been completely forgotten were it not for the fact that church music and most folk tunes were modal. And, fortunately, they continued to be taught in some conservatories of music. Revival of the modes by romantic composers was just a beginning. About 1890 Debussy, followed by many twentieth century composers, began using them.

The pentatonic, wholetone, dodecuple and various synthetic scales also attracted composers who were continually searching for materials that would lead them away from the cliches of the major-minor system. The ensuing section contains a discussion of these scales as well as the church modes. The general subject of tonality and modality is taken up in Chapter 4.

Not listed separately in the various lists which follow is the book *Adventures in Modes and Keys* by Glenn Mack. It is a most significant contribution to the late elementary or early intermediate level, for it consists of fifty short studies based upon all the modes, as well as major and minor, Hungarian, pentatonic, whole tone, chromatic and twelve-tone scales. Brief explanations are given. (Polytonality, ostinato and asymmetric meters are utilized incidentally.)

At this juncture it is important to realize that, though the sound of a piece is largely determined by its scale basis, it will always be true of the phenomenon of musical creativity that the *analysis* of its theoretical basis *follows* rather than precedes it. This means that a composer does *not* "program" his intuition and imagination to produce music based upon a prescribed scale. Instead, a scale is *derived* from the tones of a melody. New or synthetic scales come into being this way. Despite this order of events, it *is* instructive for the pianist to examine the intervallic structures of the new scales and learn to recognize them aurally, for the hand must gradually learn the "feel" of these new patterns, a task made considerably easier when the ear becomes trained to these unfamiliar sounds and can direct the fingers accurately.

Church Modes

The church modes can be grouped into two categories—those that sound major because of a *major* third between the first and third degrees, and those that sound minor because of a *minor* third between the first and third degrees. Classifying them in this way and learning the tones that distinguish them from a major or minor scale will aid in their recognition. For it is characteristic of the modern treatment of modes that they make only fleeting appearances or that they frequently interchange throughout the course of a melody making them elusive and difficult to identify. In other instances, however, a complete melody may adhere to one mode.

The three major-sounding modes are Ionian (same as major), Lydian (major with raised fourth) and Mixolydian (major with lowered seventh). The remaining four are in the minor category. Comparing them with the natural minor scale, the Dorian contains a raised sixth; the Phrygian, a lowered second; Aeolian, same as natural minor; and Locrian, a lowered second and fifth. (As previously mentioned, the Locrian mode was never actually used because the diminished tonic chord was considered too unstable to function as a point of rest. Though less common than the others, it *is* found in contemporary music.) It was when these distinctive tones, indicated by brackets in Examples 1 and 2, were "corrected" in the sixteenth and seventeenth centuries by an accidental that the modes lost their uniqueness and dwindled down to two—Ionian and Aeolian, better known as major and minor.

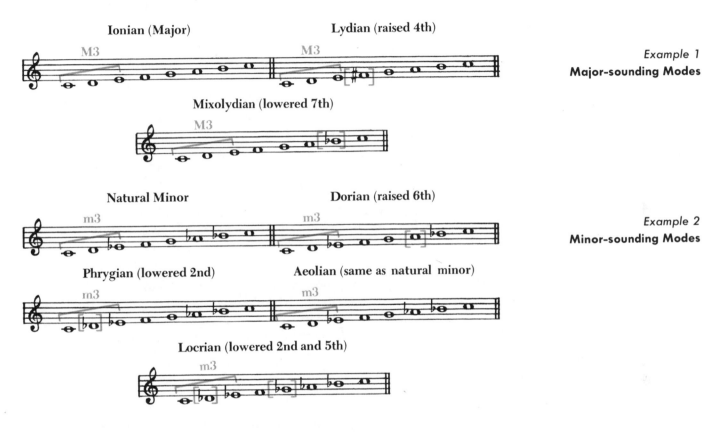

Example 1
Major-sounding Modes

Example 2
Minor-sounding Modes

Originally the modes were constructed on the white notes of the C major scale accordingly: Ionian, C to C; Dorian, D to D; Phrygian, E to E; Lydian, F to F; Mixolydian, G to G; Aeolian, A to A; and Locrian, B to B.

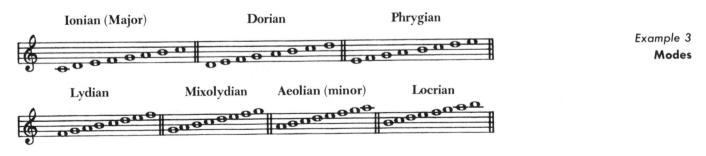

Example 3
Modes

However, modern usage allows them to occur on any degree of the scale.

Example 4
Transposed Modes

Key signatures vary. For prolonged modal passages there are two possibilities. To illustrate, D Mixolydian could have a D major signature of two sharps with an accidental showing the lowered seventh, C♮; or the G major signature, which eliminates the need for an accidental.

Melody in D Mixolydian (D Major key signature)

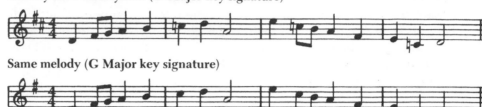

Same melody (G Major key signature)

Example 5
Modal Key Signatures

When minor-sounding modes interchange or are interpolated in a minor passage, the signature of the minor mode is commonly used. Similarly, with major-sounding modes, the signature of the major mode is used.

Example 6
Modal Interchange

g minor   g Dorian   g Phrygian

Examples of modal writing abound in elementary and intermediate piano literature where folk-like melodies and thin, uncomplicated textures are most appropriate.

In the lists which follow, *Six Modal Miniatures* by Everett Stevens and *In the Mode* edited by Mary Elizabeth Clark deserve special attention. Both are on the preparatory level and contain explanations of the various modes, though it is left to the performer to locate and identify them as they occur.

Examples of Dorian

ELEMENTARY
Bartok, Bela   *The First Term at the Piano,* #15 ("Wedding Song")
Bartok, Bela   *For Children, Vol. I,* #3
Bartok, Bela   *For Children, Vol. I,* #10
Bartok, Bela   *For Children, Vol. I,* #14
Bartok, Bela   *Mikrokosmos, Vol. I,* #12
Bartok, Bela   *Mikrokosmos, Vol. I,* #32 ("In Dorian Mode")
Bartok, Bela   *Mikrokosmos, Vol. II,* #45
Bartok, Bela   *Mikrokosmos, Vol. II,* #65
Bartok, Bela   *Ten Easy Pieces,* "Dance of the Slovaks"
Contemporary Collection, Revised Edition, "Folk Song" by Fred Ziller
Contemporary Collection, Revised Edition, "Rain in the Afternoon" by Wesley Wehr
Contemporary Collection, Revised Edition, "A Shepherd Plays" by T. Salutrinskaya
Kabalevsky, Dmitri   *24 Little Pieces for Children Op. 39,* #8
Masters of Our Day, "The Bell" by Howard Hanson
Siegmeister, Elie   *American Kaleidoscope,* "Old Time Dance"
Siegmeister, Elie   *American Kaleidoscope,* "Song of the Dark Woods"
Stevens, Everett   *Six Modal Miniatures,* "Forlana"
Stevens, Everett   *Six Modal Miniatures,* "Highland Hornpipe"
Stevens, Everett   *Six Modal Miniatures,* "Lonesome Trail"
Stravinsky, Soulima   *Piano Music for Children, Vol. I,* #12 ("Pastoral tune")

INTERMEDIATE

Bartok, Bela   *Mikrokosmos, Vol. III,* #77
Bartok, Bela   *Mikrokosmos, Vol. III,* #87
Bartok, Bela   *Roumanian Folk Dances,* #1
°Bartok, Bela   *Roumanian Folk Dances,* #2
Bartok, Bela   *Sonatina,* Second Movement
Bartok, Bela   *Three Hungarian Folk-Tunes,* #2
Bloch, Ernest   *Enfantines,* #7 ("Pastorale")
°Bloch, Ernest   *Enfantines,* #10 ("Dream")
°Casella, Alfredo   *11 Children's Pieces,* VI ("Siciliana")
Contemporary Collection, Revised Edition, "Three Short Pieces," II by
    Hugh Aitken
Fuleihan, Anis   *Ionian Pentagon,* #5 (middle)
In the Mode, "Christmas Comes Anew" by Ruth Perdew
In the Mode, "Grecian Lullaby" by Anne Shannon Demarest
In the Mode, "Happiness" by D. Jaeger Brew
In the Mode, "Merrymaking" (duet) by Ruth Perdew
Kabalevsky, Dmitri   *Children's Pieces Op. 27,* "A Little Fairy Tale"
Kabalevsky, Dmitri   *Children's Pieces Op. 27,* "Sonatina"
Kabalevsky, Dmitri   *Sonatina Op. 13 No. 1,* First and Third Move-
    ments
Masters of Our Day, "Dance of the Warriors" by Howard Hanson
Masters of Our Day, "Song After Sundown" by Randall Thompson
Stravinsky, Soulima   *Six Sonatinas,* "Sonatina Sesta," Second Move-
    ment
Tansman, Alexandre   *Pour les Enfants, 4th Set,* #1 ("An Old Tale")

ADVANCED

Chavez, Carlos   *Ten Preludes,* #2
Chavez, Carlos   *Ten Preludes,* #9
Gershwin, George   *Preludes for Piano,* III (Dorian sixth on tonic)
Hindemith, Paul   *Sonata No. 2,* First Movement
Kennan, Kent   *Three Preludes,* #2 (cadence)
Shostakovitch, Dmitri   *24 Preludes and Fugues Op. 87,* #16
Tcherepnin, Alexander   *Bagatelles Op. 5,* #2 (middle)
Tcherepnin, Alexander   *Bagatelles Op. 5,* #5

ELEMENTARY   ***Examples of Phrygian***

Adler, Samuel   *Gradus I,* #4
Adler, Samuel   *Gradus I,* #14
Bartok, Bela   *Mikrokosmos, Vol. I,* #7
Bartok, Bela   *Mikrokosmos, Vol. I,* #34 ("Phrygian Mode")
Bartok, Bela   *Mikrokosmos, Vol. II,* #44
Bartok, Bela   *Mikrokosmos, Vol. II,* Appendix 6b
Dello Joio, Norman   *Suite for the Young,* #5 ("Lullaby") (cadence)
Masters of Our Day, "The Irishman Dances" by Henry Cowell
Stevens, Everett   *Six Modal Miniatures,* "County Fair"

INTERMEDIATE

American Composers of Today, "The Small Sad Sparrow" by Vivian
    Fine
Bartok, Bela   *Mikrokosmos, Vol. IV,* #120
°Bloch, Ernest   *Enfantines,* #8 ("Rainy Day")
Casella, Alfredo   *11 Children's Pieces,* II ("Valse Diatonique") (middle)
Hindemith, Paul   *Easy Five-Tone Pieces,* #1
Hindemith, Paul   *Easy Five-Tone Pieces,* #3
Hindemith, Paul   *Easy Five-Tone Pieces,* #4
Hindemith, Paul   *Easy Five-Tone Pieces,* #8
Hindemith, Paul   *Easy Five-Tone Pieces,* #9
Hindemith, Paul   *Easy Five-Tone Pieces,* #12
In the Mode, "Desert Caravan" by Billie Ferrell

°denotes musical example

In the Mode, "Moods" by Ruth Perdew
In the Mode, "Promenade" by D. Jaeger Bres
Kabalevsky, Dmitri   *Children's Pieces Op. 27*, "Novelette"
Kabalevsky, Dmitri   *Children's Pieces Op. 27*, "Sad Little Tale"
Khachaturian, Aram   *Adventures of Ivan*, #1 ("Ivan Sings")
(cadences)

ADVANCED

Chavez, Carlos   *Ten Preludes*, #1
Fuleihan, Anis   *Sonatina No. 2*, Second Movement
Hindemith, Paul   *Sonata No. 2*, First and Third Movements
Kabalevsky, Dmitri   *24 Preludes Op. 38*, #11
Kabalevsky, Dmitri   *24 Preludes Op. 38*, #12
Kabalevsky, Dmitri   *24 Preludes Op. 38*, #13 (cadences)
Kennan, Kent   *Three Preludes*, #3 (melodic fragments)
Prokofiev, Serge   *Visions Fugitives Op. 22*, #16
Tcherepnin, Alexander   *Bagatelles Op. 5*, #4

Examples of Lydian

ELEMENTARY

Bartok, Bela   *Mikrokosmos, Vol. II*, #37 ("Lydian Mode")
Bartok, Bela   *Mikrokosmos, Vol. II*, #45
Bartok, Bela   *Mikrokosmos, Vol. II*, #50
Bartok, Bela   *Mikrokosmos, Vol. II*, #55 ("Triplets in Lydian Mode"—
duet)
Contemporary Collection, Revised Edition, "March" by Fred Ziller
Contemporary Collection, Revised Edition, "Slavic Dance" by David
Kraehenbuehl
Frackenpohl, Arthur   *Circus Parade*, #4 ("Jig")
Frackenpohl, Arthur   *Circus Parade*, #11 ("Lydian Tune")
Persichetti, Vincent   *Parades for Piano*, "March"
Siegmeister, Elie   *American Kaleidoscope*, "Fairy Tale"
Stevens, Everett   *Six Modal Miniatures*, "Highland Hornpipe"
Stravinsky, Igor   *Les Cinq Doigts (The Five Fingers)*, #7 (middle)
Stravinsky, Soulima   *Piano Music for Children, Vol. I*, #16 ("Tri-
cycle") (blend of C Lydian and A Dorian)
Stravinsky, Soulima   *Piano Music for Children, Vol. II*, #20 ("First
date") (slight effects)

INTERMEDIATE

Bartok, Bela   *For Children, Vol. II*, #9
Bartok, Bela   *For Children, Vol. II*, #20
Bartok, Bela   *Mikrokosmos, Vol. III*, #75
Bartok, Bela   *Mikrokosmos, Vol. III*, #77
Bartok, Bela   *Mikrokosmos, Vol. III*, #82
Bartok, Bela   *Mikrokosmos, Vol. V*, #130
Bartok, Bela   *Roumanian Folk Dances*, #5
Bartok, Bela   *Roumanian Folk Dances*, #6
Bartok, Bela   *Sonatina*, Second and Third Movements
Casella, Alfredo   *11 Children's Pieces*, I ("Preludio")
Casella, Alfredo   *11 Children's Pieces*, IV ("Bolero")
°Casella, Alfredo   *11 Children's Pieces*, VI ("Siciliana") (see Example 9)
Casella, Alfredo   *11 Children's Pieces*, VII ("Giga")
Casella, Alfredo   *11 Children's Pieces*, VIII ("Minuetto")
Casella, Alfredo   *11 Children's Pieces*, X ("Berceuse")
Contemporary Collection, Revised Edition, "Scherzo" by Dennis Riley
Contemporary Collection, Revised Edition, "Three Short Pieces," I
by Hugh Aitken
Creston, Paul   *Five Little Dances*, "Pastoral Dance"
Creston, Paul   *Five Little Dances*, "Rustic Dance"
Creston, Paul   *Five Little Dances*, "Toy Dance"
Hindemith, Paul   *Easy Five-Tone Pieces*, #6
Hindemith, Paul   *Easy Five-Tone Pieces*, #9
In the Mode, "March of the Pachyderms" (duet) by Anne Shannon
Demarest

°Kabalevsky, Dmitri *Children's Pieces Op. 27,* "Sonatina"
Prokofiev, Serge *Four Pieces Op. 32,* "Minuet" (cadences)
Stravinsky, Soulima *Six Sonatinas,* "Sonatina Prima," Third
  Movement

ADVANCED

Bartok, Bela *Three Rondos* (melodic fragments in all three)
Chavez, Carlos *Ten Preludes,* #7
Chavez, Carlos *Ten Preludes,* #8
Fuleihan, Anis *Sonatina No. 2,* Last Movement
Hindemith, Paul *Sonata No. 2,* "Rondo"
Kennan, Kent *Three Preludes,* #1 (melodic fragments)

ELEMENTARY

Examples of Mixolydian

Bartok, Bela *Mikrokosmos, Vol. I,* #11
Bartok, Bela *Mikrokosmos, Vol. I,* #15
Bartok, Bela *Mikrokosmos, Vol. II,* #40
Bartok, Bela *Mikrokosmos, Vol. II,* #48 ("Mixolydian Mode")
Contemporary Collection, Revised Edition, "Bells" by Fred Ziller
Contemporary Collection, Revised Edition, "Scherzo on Tenth Avenue"
  by David Kraehenbuehl
Dello Joio, Norman *Suite for the Young,* #5 ("Lullaby")
Fletcher, Stanley *Street Scenes,* "Hello, Mr. O'Hoolihan!"
Masters of Our Day, "Fiddlin' Joe" from *Tintypes* by Douglas Moore
Shostakovitch, Dmitri *Six Children's Pieces* "The Mechanical Doll"
Siegmeister, Elie *American Kaleidoscope,* "Fairy Tale"
Stevens, Everett *Six Modal Miniatures,* "An Ancient Roundelay"
Stevens, Everett *Six Modal Miniatures,* "County Fair"
Stravinsky, Soulima *Piano Music for Children, Vol. II,* #28 ("Answering back") (some effects)

INTERMEDIATE

American Composers of Today, "Game" by Norman Cazden
American Music by Distinguished Composers, Book 2, "Sway Dance"
  by Henry Cowell
Bartok, Bela *For Children, Vol. I,* #18
Bartok, Bela *For Children, Vol. I,* #37
Bartok, Bela *Mikrokosmos, Vol. III,* #69 ("Chord Study")
Bartok, Bela *Mikrokosmos, Vol. III,* #73
Bartok, Bela *Mikrokosmos, Vol. III,* #83
Bartok, Bela *Mikrokosmos, Vol. IV,* #102 ("Harmonics")
Bartok, Bela *Mikrokosmos, Vol. IV,* #120
Bartok, Bela *Mikrokosmos, Vol. V,* #126 ("Change of Time")
Bartok, Bela *Roumanian Folk Dances,* #5 (ending)
Bartok, Bela *Roumanian Folk Dances,* #6 (ending)
Bartok, Bela *Sonatina,* Third Movement
Bartok, Bela *Three Hungarian Folk-Tunes,* #1
Bartok, Bela *Three Hungarian Folk-Tunes,* #3
°*In the Mode,* "Old Joe Clark" by Ruth Perdew
In the Mode, "Ping Pong" by Anne Shannon Demarest
In the Mode, "Splash!" by Ruth Perdew

ADVANCED

Bartok, Bela *Mikrokosmos, Vol. VI,* #153 (final chord)
Chavez, Carlos *Ten Preludes,* #6
Chavez, Carlos *Ten Preludes,* #9 (middle)

ELEMENTARY

Examples of Aeolian

Adler, Samuel *Gradus I,* #4
Bartok, Bela *The First Term at the Piano,* #12 ("Swineherd's Dance")
Bartok, Bela *Mikrokosmos, Vol. I,* #5

Bartok, Bela   *Mikrokosmos, Vol. I,* #8
Contemporary Collection, Revised Edition, "Dusk" by Stanley Fletcher
Kabalevsky, Dmitri   *24 Little Pieces for Children Op. 39,* #22
Stevens, Everett   *Six Modal Miniatures,* "An Ancient Roundelay"
Stevens, Everett   *Six Modal Miniatures,* "Forlana"
Stevens, Everett   *Six Modal Miniatures,* "Lonesome Trail"
Stevens. Everett   *Six Modal Miniatures,* "Quilting Party"
Stravinsky, Igor   *Les Cinq Doigts (The Five Fingers),* #4
Stravinsky, Igor   *Les Cinq Doigts (The Five Fingers),* #5
Stravinsky, Soulima   *Piano Music for Children, Vol. I,* #13 ("Wistful")
Stravinsky, Soulima   *Piano Music for Children, Vol. I,* #18 ("On the way to school")

INTERMEDIATE

American Music by Distinguished Composers, Book 2, "Sway Dance" by Henry Cowell
Bartok, Bela   *For Children, Vol. I,* #21
Bartok, Bela   *Sonatina,* Second Movement
Bartok, Bela   *Ten Easy Pieces,* "Evening in the Country"
Bloch, Ernest   *Enfantines,* #1 ("Lullaby")
Bloch, Ernest   *Enfantines,* #2 ("The Joyous Party")
Casella, Alfredo   *11 Children's Pieces,* VIII ("Minuetto")
Contemporary Collection, Revised Edition, "Dirge" by William Pottebaum
Creston, Paul   *Five Little Dances,* "Pastoral Dance"
Fuleihan, Anis   *Ionian Pentagon,* #5
Kabalevsky, Dmitri   *Children's Pieces Op. 27,* "Ballad"
°Kabalevsky, Dmitri   *Children's Pieces Op. 27,* "Sonatina"
Kabalevsky, Dmitri   *Children's Pieces Op. 27,* "Toccatina"
Kabalevsky, Dmitri   *Sonatina Op. 13 No. 1,* Second Movement
Masters of Our Day, "The Bell" by Howard Hanson
Masters of Our Day, "The Irishman Dances" by Henry Cowell
Scott, Cyril   *Pastoral Suite,* "Passacaglia"
Stravinsky, Soulima   *Six Sonatinas,* "Sonatina Prima," Second Movement
Stravinsky, Soulima   *Six Sonatinas,* "Sonatina Quarta" ("Plainchant")
Tansman, Alexandre   *Pour les Enfants, 4th Set,* #2 ("Rocking Horse")
Tansman, Alexandre   *Pour les Enfants, 4th Set,* #5 ("In a Venetian Gondola")

ADVANCED

Chavez, Carlos   *Ten Preludes,* #5
Tcherepnin, Alexander   *Bagatelles Op. 5,* #1
Tcherepnin, Alexander   *Bagatelles Op. 5,* #9
Villa-Lobos, Heitor   *The Three Maries,* "Mintika"

Examples of Locrian

ELEMENTARY

Adler, Samuel   *Gradus I,* #7
Bartok, Bela   *Mikrokosmos, Vol. II,* #63
Bartok, Bela   *Mikrokosmos, Vol. II,* Appendix 6a
Bartok, Bela   *Mikrokosmos, Vol. II,* Appendix 7

INTERMEDIATE

Bartok, Bela   *Mikrokosmos, Vol. V,* #132
Horizons, Book 1, "In Locrian Mode" by C. Elliott
°*In the Mode,* "Rock Bound Coast" by Eloise Ristad

ADVANCED

Chavez, Carlos   *Ten Preludes,* #4

Example 7
BARTOK
Roumanian Folk Dances,
#2
(m. 1-5)

Excerpt from *Roumanian Folk Dances,* by BELA BARTOK. ' Copyright 1918 by Universal Edition. Copyright and renewal assigned to Boosey & Hawkes, Inc., for the U.S.A. Reprinted by Permission.

Example 8
BLOCH
Enfantines, **#10**
("Dream")
(m. 1-4)

Excerpt from "Dream" from *Enfantines* by ERNEST BLOCH. ' Copyright MCMXXIV by Carl Fischer, Inc., New York. International Copyright Secured. Used by Permission.

Example 9
CASELLA
11 Children's Pieces, VI
("Siciliana")
(m. 1-15)

Excerpt from *11 Children's Pieces* by ALFREDO CASELLA. ' Copyright 1921 by Universal Edition A.G., Wein. Renewed 1949. Used by Permission of Universal Edition A.G.

Example 10
BLOCH
Enfantines, #8
("Rainy Day")
(m. 1-8)

Andante con moto (♩=112)   [Phrygian]

p dolce

Example 11
KABALEVSKY
Children's Pieces Op. 27
"Sonatina"
(m. 30-34)

[Lydian]

Example 12
PERDEW
Old Joe Clark
(m. 1-8)

Lively   [Mixolydian]

mp

Example 13
KABALEVSKY
Children's Pieces Op. 27
"Sonatina"
(m. 1-14)

Example 14
RISTAD
Rock Bound Coast
(m. 21-28)

Pentatonic and Wholetone Scales

One of the oldest scales, as primitive folksongs reveal, is the *pentatonic*. Any series of five tones may correctly be given this name but the most common arrangement is that represented by the black notes on the keyboard, any one of which may be designated as the tonic.

The Pentatonic Scale showing each tone as "tonic"

Example 15
Pentatonic Scale

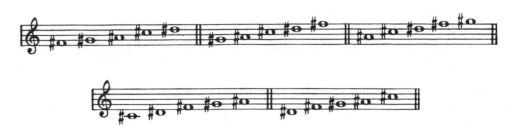

The tune, "Auld Lang Syne" and the principal theme of the second movement of Mendelssohn's *Scotch Symphony* are both based on this scale.

Example 16
Pentatonic Scale Melodies

a.   "Auld Lang Syne"

b.   Mendelssohn: *Symphony No. 3 in A Minor Op. 56* ("Scotch Symphony"), Second Movement

The most well-known hexatonic or six-note scale is the *wholetone*. It is associated with Debussy and Impressionism but actually plays a very minor role in that style of music. Only two are possible (totaling the twelve different tones of the octave), constructed on adjacent half steps. All other notations will result in one of these two sounds.

Example 17
Wholetone Scale

These two non-Western scales—pentatonic and wholetone—have much in common. Neither one contains half steps, so all tones may be made to sound simultaneously, producing a static or atmospheric effect. When used melodically, they

are often harmonized by foreign chords to give needed variety and color. In addition, they are both harmonically monotonous and are, therefore, most effective in short passages where they offer striking contrast to the prevailing character. Such is the case in Debussy's "Voiles" from *Preludes, Book 1*, where a pentatonic passage suddenly disturbs the tranquillity of the wholetone fabric, generates a hasty climax and then disappears.

Example 18
DEBUSSY
Preludes, Book 1, #2
("Voiles")
(m. 38-48)

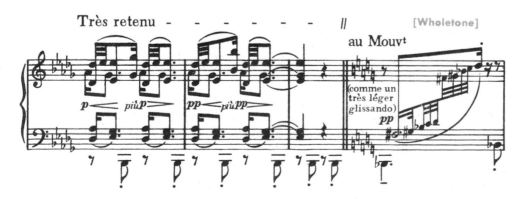

Example 22
IVEY
Magic Circles
(m. 1-9)

Excerpt from *Magic Circles* by JEAN E. IVEY. Reprinted from *Contemporary Collection*, Revised Edition. ' Copyright 1974 by Summy-Birchard Company, Evanston, Illinois. All Rights Reserved. Used by Permission.

Dodecuple Scale

From its notational appearance, the *dodecuple* (or duodecuple) scale resembles the familiar chromatic scale.

Example 23
Chromatic and Dodecuple Scales

a. The Chromatic Scale (**several spellings are possible**)

b. The Dodecuple Scale (**any spelling is possible**)

But it differs functionally in that all twelve tones are equally important. There is no hierarchy that elevates one note above another as in tonal or modal music where the tonic is the center of gravity, the point of departure and return. Nor is there any distinction between diatonic and chromatic or major and minor. The chromatic scale always has a major or minor (less frequently modal) scale as its basis and is, therefore, associated with traditional tonal music. In contrast, the dodecuple scale is derived from *atonal* music whether serial or free. By definition, *atonality* means the absence of tonality and is achieved by avoiding any functional relationship among the twelve tones, all of which are used freely and independently of each other.

To illustrate, Example 24 contains two melodies reflecting these scales. The chromatic Chopin melody is clearly heard in e minor due to the emphasis on the tonic in measures twenty-two and twenty-five, and the resolution of the leading tone, D♯ to E, in measures twenty-two and twenty-three. But the dodecaphonic melody has no point of gravitation.

Example 24
**Chromatic and Dodecuple
Scale Melodies**

Tonal–Chromatic Melody (using 11 different tones); key signature is used
Chopin: *Mazurka #11, Op. 17 No. 2* (m. 22-25)

Atonal–Dodecaphonic Melody (using 11 different tones); no key signature

Whether this dodecaphonic melody represents *expanded tonality* (ends on a tonic) or *free atonality* (no tonic) depends upon its harmony and final cadence. (The general subject of tonality is taken up in Chapter 4.)

Serial atonality, on the other hand, completely eradicates the possibility of an axis, for the twelve tones are pre-arranged by the composer into a set order or *row* which becomes the basis of both melodic and harmonic evolution. (According to Peter Hansen, "mathematicians have calculated that there are 479,001,600 different tone-rows available."[4]) Tones appear only in this order unless a transformation of the row occurs—inversion, retrograde, retrograde inversion and transposition. The row, thus, becomes a formal element which, unfortunately for the listener, is perceived visually more than aurally.

Example 25
**Twelve-Tone Row
Transformations**

Row

Inversion

Retrograde

Retrograde Inversion

Transposition

---

[4]Peter Hansen, *An Introduction to Twentieth Century Music*, p. 187.

Example 26 illustrates two melodies based on this row.

Example 26
Serial Melodies

Understanding the properties of the dodecuple scale and how it differs from the chromatic is all that is needful at this point. All of the pieces listed below, except those by Diamond and Schoenberg, contain explanatory material and, therefore, serve as a good introduction to dodecaphonic music. Other examples are given in Chapter 4 where the study of atonality is pursued.

Examples of Free and Serial Atonality

INTERMEDIATE

Adler, Samuel *Gradus II*, #8
Adler, Samuel *Gradus II*, #9
Adler, Samuel *Gradus II*, #10
Adler, Samuel *Gradus II*, #11
Contemporary Collection, Revised Edition, "Night Shadows" by Ihor Bilohrud (serial)
Diamond, David *Alone at the Piano, Book 2*, #4 (all the pieces are free atonality)
°Krenek, Ernst *12 Short Piano Pieces Op. 83*, #3 ("Walking on a Stormy Day") (all the pieces are serial atonality)
°Schoenberg, Arnold *6 Kleine Klavierstucke Op. 19*, IV (all the pieces are free atonality)
°Starer, Robert *Sketches in Color*, #5 ("Grey") (serial)

ADVANCED

Riegger, Wallingford *New and Old*, #4 ("The Twelve Tones") (serial)
Riegger, Wallingford *New and Old*, #5 ("Shifted Rhythm") (serial)
Riegger, Wallingford *New and Old*, #6 ("Twelve Upside Down") (serial)

Excerpt from *12 Short Piano Pieces* Op. 83, by ERNST KRENEK. ' Copyright by G. Schirmer, Inc. Used by Permission.

Excerpt from *6 Kleine Klavierstucke* Op. 19 by ARNOLD SCHOENBERG. ' Copyright 1913 by Universal Edition. Copyright renewed 1940 by Arnold Schoenberg. Used by Permission of Belmont Music Publishers, Los Angeles, California, 90049.

Example 28
SCHOENBERG
6 Kleine Klavierstucke
Op. 19, IV
(m. 1-6)

Excerpt from *Sketches in Color* by ROBERT STARER. ' Copyright 1964 by MCA Music, a division of MCA, Inc., New York, N.Y. Used by Permission. All Rights Reserved.

Example 29
STARER
Sketches in Color, # 5
("Grey")
(m. 1-8)

Melody   37

Synthetic Scales

Among the synthetic scales found in contemporary music are several that have become so commonly used that they have been given names. Three of the more prominent ones are shown in the next example—*Hungarian minor* (or Gypsy), *Spanish* and *Bagpipe*.

Example 30
Synthetic Scales

The Hungarian mode, identified by two augmented seconds, is used primarily in melodies. Chopin employed it in *Mazurkas* #5, 14, 38 and 47.

Example 31
CHOPIN
Mazurka #14, Op. 24
No. 1
(m. 1-8)

In the Spanish mode the tonic triad is major, preceding or against which a descending major or minor third and lowered second pass melodically. The diminished v°7 and minor vii7 resolving to a major I are characteristic cadence sounds.

Example 32
Progressions in the Spanish Mode

Comparing the Bagpipe scale with the major, the fourth tone is slightly sharp and the seventh, a bit flat. Since quarter tones are impossible on the piano, composers such as Bartok have resorted to raising the fourth and lowering the seventh, a combination of the Lydian and Mixolydian modes, to approximate the scale produced by a bagpipe. The left hand carries a drone bass accompaniment as seen in this next example.

Example 33
BARTOK
Sonatina
First Movement
("Bagpipe")
(m. 1-8)

Excerpt from *Sonatina* by BELA BARTOK. Used by Permission of Edwin F. Kalmus.

Not all synthetic scales, however, have names; it is the prerogative of the composer to create music whose scale resource is truly synthetic or original. One does not play Bartok for very long before making this discovery. Such music often requires a new key signature. There are even instances where the pianist must adjust to reading two different key signatures simultaneously, and sometimes they are both atypical, as in the following example.

Example 34
BARTOK
Mikrokosmos, Vol. IV,
#99
(m. 1-4)

Excerpt from *Mikrokosmos, Vol. IV* by BELA BARTOK. © Copyright 1940 by Hawkes & Son (London) Ltd., Renewed 1967. Reprinted by Permission of Boosey & Hawkes, Inc.

ELEMENTARY
    Bartok, Bela   *Mikrokosmos, Vol. I,* #10
    Bartok, Bela   *Mikrokosmos, Vol. I,* #25 (new key signatures)
    Bartok, Bela   *Mikrokosmos, Vol. II,* #41 (bagpipe)
    Bartok, Bela   *Mikrokosmos, Vol. II,* #52 (bagpipe)
    Bartok, Bela   *Mikrokosmos, Vol. II,* #58
    °*Contempo 1*, "Hungarian Festival" by Ruth Perdew (Hungarian)

Examples of Synthetic Scales

Example 35
PERDEW
Hungarian Festival
(m. 1-8)

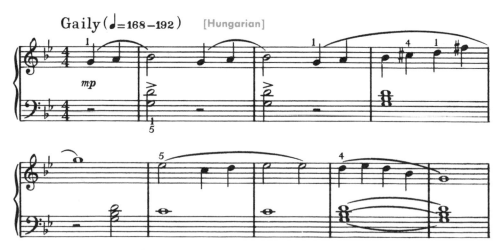

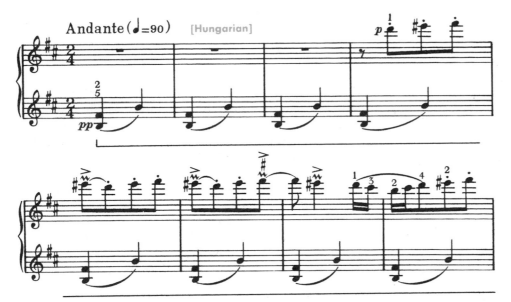

Example 36
BARTOK
Roumanian Folk Dances,
 # 3
(m. 1-8)

Excerpt from *Roumanian Folk Dances* by BELA BARTOK. ° Copyright 1918 by Universal Edition. Copyright and renewal assigned to Boosey & Hawkes, Inc., for the U.S.A. Reprinted by Permission.

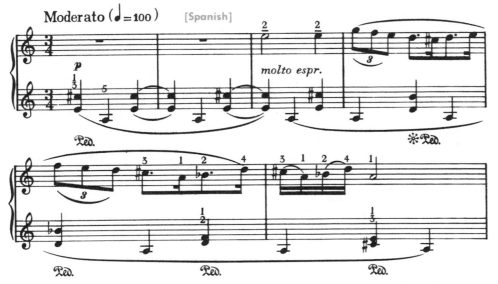

Example 37
BARTOK
Roumanian Folk Dances,
 # 4
(m. 1-6)

Excerpt from *Roumanian Folk Dances* by BELA BARTOK. ° Copyright 1918 by Universal Edition. Copyright and renewal assigned to Boosey & Hawkes, Inc., for the U.S.A. Reprinted by Permission.

Example 38
CASELLA
11 Children's Pieces, IV
("Bolero")
(m. 1-6)

Excerpt from *11 Children's Pieces* by ALFREDO CASELLA. ° Copyright 1921 by Universal Edition A. G., Wein. Renewed 1949. Used by Permission of Universal Edition A.G.

Melody   41

Pitch Characteristics

The attributes of traditional tonal melody, spelled out in the beginning of the chapter, were seen to be primarily vocal in character. Not all of these qualities have been abandoned by twentieth century composers, for many themes exist which adhere to the ingratiating curves and tonal stability of the classic-romantic idiom. Furthermore, instances occur where composers have made a conscious attempt to create medieval-like melodies of plainsong derivation with winsome simplicity and gently undulating contour. Norman Dello Joio begins his *Piano Sonata No. 3* with a Gregorian tune or plainchant (upon which he bases a set of variations) and concludes his *Suite for the Young* with a chorale chant; the second movement of Soulima Stravinsky's *Sonatina Quarta* is also a plainchant. Robert Starer's fifth *Vignette* is a chorale, as is the second movement of Bartok's *Piano Concerto No. 3*.

Example 39
DELLO JOIO
Piano Sonata No. 3
First Movement
(m. 1-5a)

Excerpt from *Piano Sonata No. 3* by NORMAN DELLO JOIO. ' Copyright MCMXLVIII by Carl Fischer, Inc., New York. International Copyright Secured. Used by Permission.

Example 40
STRAVINSKY
Six Sonatinas
"Sonatina Quarta"
Second Movement
(m. 1-14)

Excerpt from *Six Sonatinas for Young Pianists* (P 6590a/b) by SOULIMA STRAVINSKY. ' Copyright 1967 by C. F. Peters Corporation, 373 Park Avenue South, New York, New York 10016. Reprint permission granted by the publisher.

Example 41
STARER
Seven Vignettes, V
("Chorale")
(m. 1-4)

Excerpt from *Seven Vignettes for Piano* by ROBERT STARER. ℗ Copyright MCML by MCA Music, a division of MCA, Inc., New York, N.Y. Used by Permission. All Rights Reserved.

But this type of melody does not require special attention. Rather, it is the innovative, seemingly incoherent twentieth century tune which cries out for acceptance and understanding.

Incredible as it may appear at times, most recent composers *still* regard melody as the primary element in music. Prokofiev admits that one of his biggest problems and challenges as a composer was to write a melody that would, on the one hand, be *understandable* to the average listener and at the same time be *original.*[5] Not an easy task! It is the performer's dual responsibility, then, to approach modern music with an attitude of trust that the composer has not just flung notes haphazardly on the page without due concern for order and meaning; and to gain an understanding of its various unique features so that they may be heard and reckoned upon as legitimate constituents of unity, replacing the old familiar trademarks discussed earlier.

The salient characteristics of contemporary melody are extended range, limited range (turning around within a very small compass of notes), exploitation of extremely high and low registers, angular and disjointed lines caused by numerous wide and dissonant leaps (sevenths, ninths, tritones), and successive skips in the same direction often outlining non-tertial chords (consecutive leaps of fourths and fifths). Most of these features are contained in the following illustrations.

Example 42
**Extended Range and
Wide Leaps**

Example 43
Limited Range

Example 44
**Successive Skips and
Angular Line**

No doubt, the reader has concluded from these samples that contemporary melody is unsingable. This is a fact, of course, not an accusation. For, despite the evidence that it is non-vocal, grotesque and difficult to remember, it has proven itself to be a genuine artistic expression reflective of modern times.

ELEMENTARY

    Bartok, Bela   *Mikrokosmos, Vol. II,* #49
    Bartok, Bela   *Mikrokosmos, Vol. II,* #50
    Bartok, Bela   *Mikrokosmos, Vol. II,* #51
    Bartok, Bela   *Mikrokosmos, Vol. II,* #58
    Bartok, Bela   *Mikrokosmos, Vol. II,* #63 (limited)
 °Stravinsky, Igor   *Les Cinq Doigts (The Five Fingers),* #2 (all eight pieces
    have limited ranges)

Examples of Range

---

[5]William W. Austin, *Music in the 20th Century,* p. 459.

INTERMEDIATE

Adler, Samuel   *Gradus II*, #3 (extended)
Bartok, Bela   *Mikrokosmos, Vol. III*, #88 (limited)
Bartok, Bela   *Mikrokosmos, Vol. IV*, #105
Bartok, Bela   *Mikrokosmos, Vol. IV*, #106
Bartok, Bela   *Mikrokosmos, Vol. IV*, #108
Bartok, Bela   *Mikrokosmos, Vol. IV*, #115 ("Bulgarian Rhythm") (limited)
Bartok, Bela   *Mikrokosmos, Vol. V*, #123
Bartok, Bela   *Mikrokosmos, Vol. V*, #124 ("Staccato") (limited)
Bartok, Bela   *Mikrokosmos, Vol. V*, #137 (low and high)
Bartok, Bela   *Sonatina*, Third Movement (limited)
Contemporary Piano Literature, Book 4, "Merry-Go-Round" by Alexander Tcherepnin (high)
Finney, Ross Lee   *32 Piano Games*, XXXII ("Winter") (high)
Goossens, Eugene   *Kaleidoscope*, "A Ghost Story" (low)
Goossens, Eugene   *Kaleidoscope*, "The Old Musical Box" (high)
Goossens, Eugene   *Kaleidoscope*, "The Punch and Judy Show" (high)
°Hindemith, Paul   *Easy Five-Tone Pieces*, #1 (all twelve pieces have limited ranges with both hands in the treble clef)
Krenek, Ernst   *12 Short Piano Pieces Op. 83*, #10 ("On the High Mountains") (high and low)
Mompou, Frederic   *Scènas d'Enfants*, "Jeux sur la Place" (limited)
°Prokofiev, Serge   *Children's Pieces Op. 65*, #6 ("Waltz") (extended)
Shostakovitch, Dmitri   *Dances of the Dolls*, #3 ("Romance")
Shostakovitch, Dmitri   *Dances of the Dolls*, #5 ("Petite Ballerina") (high)
°Shostakovitch, Dmitri   *Three Fantastic Dances*, #2 (extended)
Shostakovitch, Dmitri   *Three Fantastic Dances*, #3 (high)

ADVANCED

Bartok, Bela   *Mikrokosmos, Vol. VI*, #142 (limited)
Bartok, Bela   *Three Rondos*, II (high)
Bartok, Bela   *Three Rondos*, III (low)
Bartok, Bela   *Two Roumanian Dances Op. 8a*, #1 (low)
Shostakovitch, Dmitri   *24 Preludes Op. 34*, #9 (extended)
Stevens, Halsey   *Seventeen Piano Pieces*, "Another Waltz" (extended)
Stevens, Halsey   *Seventeen Piano Pieces*, "Hommage à Frederic Chopin"

Examples of Angular Lines, Wide and Dissonant Leaps

ELEMENTARY

Olson, Lynn Freeman   *Menagerie*, "The Sandpiper" (fourths)
Shostakovitch, Dmitri   *Six Children's Pieces*, "The Bear" (angular; wide leaps)

INTERMEDIATE

°*American Composers of Today*, "Duet" by Milton Babbitt (angular)
American Composers of Today, "Intermezzo" by Arthur Berger (angular; sevenths)
American Composers of Today, "Prelude" by Mario Castelnuovo-Tedesco
American Music by Distinguished Composers, "Prelude" by Douglas Moore (successive fourths in left hand)
Bartok, Bela   *Fourteen Bagatelles Op. 6*, #2 (angular) (or advanced level)
Bartok, Bela   *Fourteen Bagatelles Op. 6*, #6 (augmented intervals; successive fourths)
Bartok, Bela   *Fourteen Bagatelles Op. 6*, #13 (tritones)
Bartok, Bela   *Mikrokosmos, Vol. IV*, #98 ("Thumb Under") (tritones)
Bartok, Bela   *Mikrokosmos, Vol. V*, #125 ("Boating") (successive fourths)

Bartok, Bela   *Mikrokosmos, Vol. V*, #131 ("Fourths")
Bartok, Bela   *Ten Easy Pieces*, "Fight" (tritones)
Bloch, Ernest   *Enfantines*, #9 ("Teasing") (successive fourths)
Ginastera, Alberto   *12 American Preludes, Vol. I*, #2 ("Sadness") (fourths)
Krenek, Ernst   *12 Short Piano Pieces Op. 83*, #1 ("Dancing Toys") (angular)
Mompou, Frederic   *Scènas d' Enfants*, "Jeu" (tritones)
Pentland, Barbara   *Hands Across the C*, "Seashore" (fourths)
Pentland, Barbara   *Hands Across the C*, "Stretches 1 & 2" (fourths)
Pentland, Barbara   *Space Studies*, II ("From Outer Space") (angular)
Prokofiev, Serge   *Children's Pieces Op. 65*, #6 ("Waltz") (wide leaps)
Schoenberg, Arnold   *6 Kleine Klavierstucke Op. 19*, IV (angular; wide leaps)
Schuman, William   *Three Piano Moods*, "Lyrical" (angular)
Schuman, William   *Three-Score Set*, #1 (angular)
Shostakovitch, Dmitri   *Three Fantastic Dances*, #2 (successive fourths)
Toch, Ernst   *Echoes from a Small Town Op. 49*, #13 (tritones; fourths)
Toch, Ernst   *Reflections Op. 86*, #1 (angular)
Toch, Ernst   *Reflections Op. 86*, #2 (tritone melody)
Toch, Ernst   *Three Little Dances Op. 85*, #3 (non-tertial; atonal)

ADVANCED

Bartok, Bela   *Fourteen Bagatelles Op. 6*, #8 (sevenths; successive fifths)
Bartok, Bela   *Fourteen Bagatelles Op. 6*, #9 (sevenths; tritone cadence)
Bartok, Bela   *Fourteen Bagatelles Op. 6*, #10 (sevenths; tritones; successive fourths)
Bartok, Bela   *Mikrokosmos, Vol. VI*, #146 ("Ostinato") (tritones; successive fourths)
Hindemith, Paul   *Ludus Tonalis*, "Fuga secunda in G" (fourths)
Riegger, Wallingford   *New and Old*, #9 ("Dissonant Counterpoint") (angular; wide leaps)
Schoenberg, Arnold   *Klavierstucke Op. 33a* (angular; wide leaps)
Stevens, Halsey   *Seventeen Piano Pieces*, "Another Waltz"
Stevens, Halsey   *Seventeen Piano Pieces*, "Invention" (angular; wide leaps)
Stevens, Halsey   *Seventeen Piano Pieces*, "Prelude"
Webern, Anton   *Variations Op. 27*, III (wide leaps; pointillistic)

DIFFICULT

Barber, Samuel   *Nocturne* (angular)

Example 45
STRAVINSKY
Les Cinq Doigts, #2
(m. 36-45)

Excerpt from *Les Cinq Doigts* by IGOR STRAVINSKY. With kind permission of J & W Chester/Edition Wilhelm Hansen London Limited.

Example 46
HINDEMITH
Easy Five-Tone Pieces,
#1
(m. 1-5a)

Example 47
PROKOFIEV
Children's Pieces Op. 65,
#6
(**"Waltz"**)
(m. 13-24)

Example 48
SHOSTAKOVITCH
Three Fantastic Dances,
#2
(m. 1-9a)

Example 49
BABBITT
Duet
(m. 12-16a)

1. Play and study a representative sampling of the piano pieces listed.

2. For additional resource reading, see the following:

    Dallin   *Techniques of Twentieth Century Composition*, Chapters 2 through 4.

    Vincent   *The Diatonic Modes in Modern Music*, especially Chapter 30, "The Modes in the Contemporary Period."

3. Listen to the following complete works, with score if possible:

    Bloch   *Suite Modale for Flute and Piano* (modal themes)

    Debussy   *Preludes, Book 1*, #2 ("Voiles") (Note where the wholetone and pentatonic passages occur.)

    Hanson   *Symphony No. 1*, "Nordic," First Movement (Principal theme is Dorian.)

    Prokofiev   *Classical Symphony* (melodies with large compass)

    Prokofiev   *Violin Concerto No. 1 in D*, Second Movement (melodies with large compass)

    Prokofiev   *Piano Concerto No. 3 in C* (melodies with large compass)

4. Play the following piano pieces:

    Hindemith   *Easy Five-Tone Pieces* (small compass)

    Stravinsky   *Les Cinq Doigts (The Five Fingers)* (small compass)

    Krenek   *12 Short Piano Pieces Op. 83*, #1 ("Dancing Dolls") (angular melody)

    Prokofiev   *Children's Pieces Op. 65*, #6 ("Waltz") (large compass)

    Rebikov   *Les Demons s'amusent* (Play the wholetone scale which forms the basis of this piece. Could it be notated in any other way?)

5. Devise a twelve-tone row and write a melody and its transformations, as in Example 26. Using these materials, compose a melody which can be sung or played on an instrument.

6. Construct a two-part invention (or duet for voices or instruments) based upon an original synthetic scale.

7. Listen to a live demonstration of the Bagpipe.

8. Play the following works which contain modal melodies:

   a. Bach *Chorales* (numbering is from *The 371 Chorales of Johann Sebastian Bach*)
      Dorian—#180, 197
      Phrygian—#10, 16, 56, 253
      Lydian—#216
      Mixolydian—#154, 187, 288
      Aeolian—#28, 100

   b. *Oxford Book of Carols*
      Dorian—#115, 149, 159, 170, 177 (ending)
      Phrygian—#150, 173
      Mixolydian—#4 (first tune), 178 (second tune), 181, 192
      Aeolian—#102, 131, 166, 167, 176, 177, 180

   c. Chopin *Mazurkas* (modal melodic inflections)
      Phrygian—#17 (last eight measures), 26 (m. 1-8), 27 (m. 7,8,15,16,63-68), 48(m. 3-4)
      Lydian—#3 (m. 41-47), 15 (m. 21-36), 34 (m. 1-28, 53 to end), 48 (m. 37-44)
      Hungarian minor—#5 (m. 45-52), 14 (m. 6-8), 17 (m. 53-56), 49 (m. 8-9)

Chapter 2
Rhythm and Meter

Introduction

It is doubtful that any other element in music has undergone as much development in the twentieth century as rhythm, the "heartbeat" of music. Long the servant of melody and more recently harmony, it has been emancipated to enjoy a prominent role in our music today.

For the past three hundred years, composers have treated rhythm in a rather unobtrusive and predictable fashion. The average work of this period contained one meter throughout, with barlines grouping the metric patterns and denoting the regularly recurring accent on the first beat, though the degree of metric stress varied considerably from one work to another. Usually one rhythmic pattern sounded at a time and matched the metric organization of the measure; that is, accents coincided. It is true that syncopation, cross-rhythms (two against three, etc.), hemiola (a 3/4 measure in the midst of 6/8 ♩. ♩. | ♩♩♩ | ♩. ♩. ; or a large three extending over two measures of 3/4 ♩♩♩|♩♩♩|♩ ♩|♩ ♩ |♩♩♩) and an occasional asymmetric meter were tools in the hands of romantic composers, such as Beethoven, Schumann, Brahms, Tchaikovsky (the Second Movement of his *Symphony No. 6* is in 5/4), and Mussorgsky. But these appear mild when compared with the rhythmic complexities in some of the orchestral scores of this century, particularly those of Stravinsky and Bartok.

Companion to the rise of rhythmic significance has been the increased use of percussion instruments, including the piano, to accentuate the driving force of the pulsating and sometimes barbaric rhythms. In fact, there is a steady flow of compositions being written solely for percussion ensembles.

As a contrapuntal tool, different rhythmic patterns are combined, yet operate independently without their primary accents or subdivisions coinciding. This device, whose roots are in primitive non-western music, found its greatest exploitation in the ballet suite for orchestra, *The Rite of Spring*, by Igor Stravinsky. This excerpt contains a number of non-coinciding subdivisions.

Example 50
STRAVINSKY
The Rite of Spring
(m. 59-60a)

Excerpt from *The Rite of Spring* by IGOR STRAVINSKY from the Kalmus score. Used by Permission of Edwin F. Kalmus.

Alongside the extraordinary growth of rhythmic complexity has been the return to the simple, non-accented or speech rhythms of plainchant. Leon Dallin comments in his book, *Techniques of Twentieth Century Composition*, that this is probably due to the renewed interest in sixteenth century vocal polyphony[6] (see Examples 39 and 40).

---

[6]Leon Dallin, *Techniques of Twentieth Century Composition*, Second Edition, p. 104.

These two extremes found in contemporary music—rhythmic complexity and rhythmic simplicity—have this in common, the elimination of the metric accent, the strong beat at the beginning of each measure. (This is sometimes referred to disparagingly as the "tyranny of the barline.") Of course, there is much music whose rhythmic organization falls between these two positions. For, as mentioned earlier, the past has not been completely rejected by today's composers. Hindemith's penchant for triple meters probably reflects his interest in medieval music.[7]

The highly developed rhythmic texture of this century draws upon an enriched palette of devices which includes shifted accents, asymmetric meters and divisions, changing and alternating meters, prose rhythms, polymeters, ostinato and pedal point, and pulsating rhythm. No single piece of music contains them all, so it is advisable to study and play a wide spectrum of styles.

For the advanced pianist, Paul Creston has written *Six Preludes Op. 38* to illustrate various methods of rhythmic structure which he lists in the frontispiece. These are regular sub-division, irregular sub-division, overlapping, regular sub-division overlapping and irregular sub-division overlapping. The first *Prelude* is comprised of mixed methods so is not quoted here. For further explanation, refer to his book, *Principles of Rhythm*, listed in the Bibliography, Appendix C.

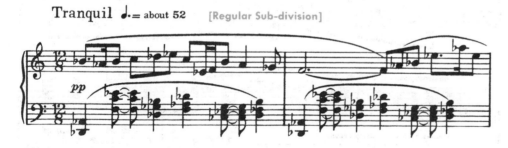

Tranquil ♩.= about 52   [Regular Sub-division]

Example 51
CRESTON
Six Preludes Op. 38, #2
(m. 1-2)

Fast ♩=126   [Regular Sub-division Overlapping]

Example 52
CRESTON
Six Preludes Op. 38, #3
(m. 1-4)

---

[7]Peter Hansen, *An Introduction to Twentieth Century Music*, p. 275.

Example 53
CRESTON
Six Preludes Op. 38, #4
(m. 1-5)

with passion

Moderately Fast ♩= 120   [Irregular Sub-division]

Example 54
CRESTON
Six Preludes Op. 38, #5
(m. 1-5)

Moderato ♩=92   [Overlapping]

p expressively

Example 55
CRESTON
Six Preludes Op. 38, #6
(m. 1-2)

Moderately Fast ♩=126   [Irregular Sub-division Overlapping]

f marked

The displacement of the primary accent of an established meter from its usual first beat of the measure to a weaker one is known as *syncopation*. A common tool in the hands of nineteenth century composers, it is the forerunner of the more complex device of *shifted accents*. Unlike syncopation, these accents usually occur in a rhythmic context devoid of regular metric pulse and are, therefore, more unpredictable. Their irregularity may be "caused" by such contour features as the beginning of a pattern; a repeated pattern or ostinato that does not coincide with the meter (could be referred to as "out-of-phase," a striking characteristic of Stravinsky's style [Examples 56a and 56b]); an arpeggiated figure whose high points are stressed at variance with the metric accent [Example 56c]; or simply by the desire of the composer to create a rough, savage rhythm.

Example 56
Shifted Accents

a.

b.

c.

INTERMEDIATE
°Bartok, Bela   *For Children, Vol. I,* #21
Bartok, Bela   *Mikrokosmos, Vol. IV,* #108
Bartok, Bela   *Mikrokosmos, Vol. V,* #122
°*Contemporary Collection,* Revised Edition, "Rain" by Dennis Riley
Pentland, Barbara   *Hands Across the C,* "Seashore"
Schuman, William   *Three Piano Moods,* "Dynamic"
Studies in 20th Century Idioms, "Rhythm and Whims" from *Intervals, Patterns, Shapes* by Brian Cherney

ADVANCED
Bartok, Bela   *Mikrokosmos, Vol. VI,* #141
Bartok, Bela   *Mikrokosmos, Vol. VI,* #146 ("Ostinato")
Bartok, Bela   *Three Rondos,* II
Bartok, Bela   *Two Roumanian Dances Op. 8a*
°Creston, Paul   *Six Preludes Op. 38,* #3 (see Example 52)
°Creston, Paul   *Six Preludes Op. 38,* #4 (see Example 53)
°Creston, Paul   *Six Preludes Op. 38,* #6 (see Example 55)
Harris, Roy   *Toccata*
Poulenc, Francis   *Mouvements Perpetuels,* #3
Prokofiev, Serge   *Visions Fugitives Op. 22,* #19

DIFFICULT
Mennin, Peter   *Five Piano Pieces,* "Toccata"

Example 57
BARTOK
For Children, Vol. I, # 21
(m. 1-4)

Excerpt from *For Children Vol. I* by BELA BARTOK. Reprinted from *Bela Bartok: An Introduction to the Composer and his Music.* ˙ Copyright 1975 by General Words and Music Company. Reprinted by Permission.

Example 58
RILEY
Rain
(m. 1-8)

Excerpt from *Rain* by DENNIS RILEY. Reprinted from *Contemporary Collection,* Revised Edition. ˙ Copyright 1974 by Summy-Birchard Company, Evanston, Illinois. All Rights Reserved. Used by Permission.

Asymmetric Meters and Divisions

Preference for new and unpredictable rhythmic patterns led composers to arrange beats into uneven (asymmetric) groups. The result was two-fold: *asymmetric meters* (5/4, 5/8, 7/4, 7/8, 11/8, 13/8, etc.) and *asymmetric divisions* of beats in conventional meters where the eighth note, or sub-pulse, remains constant (i.e., 4/4 becomes 8/8 as 3 + 3 + 2/8 or 3 + 2 + 3/8, etc.; 9/8 is divided unequally as 4 + 2 + 3, etc.). In both instances, dotted barlines are frequently used to delineate the unequal interior groupings (♩♩♩♩ ┆ ♩♩♩). Beamed eighth notes (♫ ♫ ♪) and notation of the meter (3 + 3 + 2/8) also clarify the rhythmic organization, which must be understood by the performer for a successful reading of the work or passage in the same way as pronunciation and punctuation determine the meaning of words and sentences.

These two rhythmic innovations lend fresh vitality and variety to music without adding extreme complexity. Nevertheless, an alert mind is required.

ELEMENTARY

Adler, Samuel *Gradus I,* #4 (5/4)
Adler, Samuel *Gradus I,* #7 (7/4)
Adventures in Time and Space, Vol. I, "In Orbit" by Ann Riley (5/8)
Bartok, Bela *Mikrokosmos, Vol. II,* #48 ("Mixolydian Mode") (5/4)
Contemporary Collection, Revised Edition, "Slavic Dance" by David
    Kraehenbuehl (5/4)
Contemporary Piano Literature, Book 1, "Bulldozer" by David
    Kraehenbuehl (5/4)
Diamond, David *Album for the Young, IX* ("Jostling Joe") (5/4)
Rollino, J., and Sheftel, P. *Festivities,* "Crash" (5/4)
Rollino, J., and Sheftel, P. *Festivities,* "Yoghurt"

INTERMEDIATE

Bartok, Bela *Mikrokosmos, Vol. III,* #82 (7/8)
Bartok, Bela *Mikrokosmos, Vol. IV,* #103 (5/8)
Bartok, Bela *Mikrokosmos, Vol. IV,* #113 (7/8)
°Bartok, Bela *Mikrokosmos, Vol. IV,* #115 ("Bulgarian Rhythm")
    (5/8)
Bartok, Bela *Mikrokosmos, Vol. IV,* Appendix #32
Bartok, Bela *Mikrokosmos, Vol. IV,* Appendix #33 (7/8)
Contemporary Collection, Revised Edition, "Swinging" by Blythe
    Owen (5/4)
Diamond, David *Alone at the Piano, Book 2,* #9 (7/4)
Ginastera, Alberto *12 American Preludes, Vol. I,* #5 ("In the first
    Pentatonic Minor Mode") (7/8)
Harris, Roy *Little Suite,* "Children at Play" (7/8)
Hindemith, Paul *Easy Five-Tone Pieces,* #9 (5/4; 5/8)
°Hovhaness, Alan *Mystic Flute Op. 22* (7/8 as 3+2+2/8)
Masters of Our Day, "The Young Pioneers" by Aaron Copland (7/8)
°Shostakovitch, Dmitri *24 Preludes Op. 34,* #21 (5/4)
°Starer, Robert *Sketches in Color,* #7 ("Crimson") (7/8)
Studies in 20th Century Idioms, "Ostinette" by F. R. C. Clarke (7/8)

ADVANCED

Bartok, Bela *Mikrokosmos, Vol. VI,* #140 (5/8; 7/8)
Bartok, Bela *Mikrokosmos, Vol. VI,* #149 (2+2+3/8=7/8)
Bartok, Bela *Mikrokosmos, Vol. VI,* #150 (5/8)
Creston, Paul *Six Preludes Op. 38,* #4 (5/4)
Hindemith, Paul *Ludus Tonalis,* "Fuga secunda in G" (5/8)
Kennan, Kent *Three Preludes,* #2 (5/4)
Piston, Walter *Passacaglia* (5/8)
Scriabin, Alexander *Twenty-four Preludes,* #14 (15/8)
Stevens, Halsey *Seventeen Piano Pieces,* "From a Roman Sketchbook"
    (5/8)
Tcherepnin, Alexander *Bagatelles Op. 5,* #4 (11/16; 10/16)

DIFFICULT

Mennin, Peter *Five Piano Pieces,* "Prelude" (10/8; 7/8; 5/8)
Mennin, Peter *Five Piano Pieces,* "Variation-Canzona" (5/8; 7/8)
Palmer, Robert *Toccata Ostinato* (13/8; 11/8)

**Example 59
BARTOK
Mikrokosmos, Vol. IV,
#115
("Bulgarian Rhythm")
(m. 1-3)**

Excerpt from *Mikrokosmos, Vol. IV* by BELA BARTOK. ° Copyright 1940 by Hawkes & Son (London) Ltd., Renewed 1967. Reprinted by Permission of Boosey & Hawkes, Inc.

Example 60
HOVHANESS
Mystic Flute Op. 22
(m. 1-4)

Example 61
SHOSTAKOVITCH
24 Preludes Op. 34, #21
(m. 1-9)

Example 62
STARER
Sketches in Color, #7
("Crimson")
(m. 1-8)

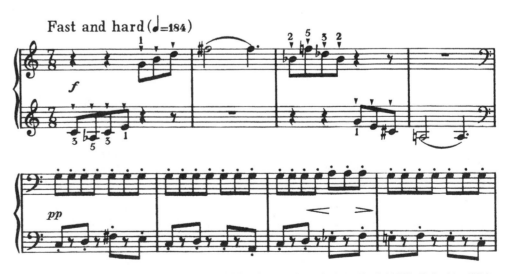

INTERMEDIATE

°Bartok, Bela *Mikrokosmos, Vol. IV,* #103 (8/8; 9/8 as 4+5/8; 3x2/8)
Contemporary Piano Literature, Book 4, "Old Tale" by Alexander
  Tcherepnin (2/4—eighth notes occur as 3+3+2 over space of two
  measures)
Pentland, Barbara *Space Studies,* IV ("Balancing Act") (8/8)
°Siegmeister, Elie *American Kaleidoscope,* "Monkey Business"
  (3+3+2 throughout)

ADVANCED

Bartok, Bela *Mikrokosmos, Vol. VI,* #140 (9/8 as 4+3+2/8; 8/8)
Bartok, Bela *Mikrokosmos, Vol. VI,* #148 (9/8)
Bartok, Bela *Mikrokosmos, Vol. VI,* #151 (8/8)
Bartok, Bela *Mikrokosmos, Vol. VI,* #152 (9/8)
Bartok, Bela *Mikrokosmos, Vol. VI,* #153 (8/8)
Creston, Paul *Six Preludes Op. 38,* #4
Khachaturian, Aram *Toccata* (two sets of 3+3+2 sixteenths in 4/4
  measure)

DIFFICULT

Mennin, Peter *Five Piano Pieces,* "Aria"
Mennin, Peter *Five Piano Pieces,* "Prelude"

Example 63
BARTOK
Mikrokosmos, Vol. IV,
#103
(m. 1-7)

Excerpt from *Mikrokosmos, Vol. IV* by BELA BARTOK. ' Copyright 1940 by Hawkes & Son (London) Ltd., Renewed 1967 Reprinted by Permission of Boosey & Hawkes, Inc.

Example 64
SIEGMEISTER
American Kaleidoscope
"Monkey Business"
(m. 1-4)

Excerpt from *American Kaleidoscope* by ELIE SIEGMEISTER. ' Copyright MCMLV by Sam Fox Publishing Company, Inc., New York, N.Y. All Rights Reserved.
International Copyright Secured Used by Permission.

Changing and Alternating Meters

One means devised by composers of this century, by which they could break away from the clutches of predictable metric pulse and achieve rhythmic variety, was to substitute *changing* (fluctuating) meters for the traditional single meter throughout a work or section of a piece. Instead of tailoring musical ideas to fit, like poetry, into successive measures of equal length, composers conceived themes with prose-like rhythms which necessitated "fluid barlines" (to borrow Persichetti's term). In this style of writing, meter becomes the servant of rhythm as well as of melody and harmony.

Changing meters are denoted either by meter signatures inserted where needed (sometimes above the staff or in large numbers between the two staves), or by no signature, but by an indication such as ♪=♪ throughout, placed at the beginning of the piece, as in Example 65. Occasionally, rare meters are found—1/2, 1/4, 3/1 and 2/4 + 1/16 (see Examples 66 and 68).

Example 65
STRAVINSKY, S.
Six Sonatinas
"Sonatina Prima"
Third Movement
(m. 1-6)

Excerpt from *Six Sonatinas for Young Pianists* by SOULIMA STRAVINSKY (P 6590a/b). ' Copyright 1967 by C. F. Peters Corporation, 373 Park Avenue South, New York, New York 10016. Reprint permission granted by the publisher.

Example 66
SCHOENBERG
Suite für Klavier Op. 25
"Praeludium"
(m. 21-24)

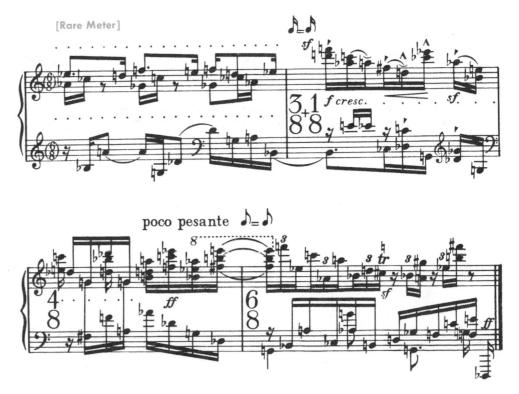

Excerpt from *Suite für Klavier Op. 25* by ARNOLD SCHOENBERG. ' Copyright 1925 by Universal Edition. Copyright renewed 1952 by Gertrude Schoenberg. Used by Permission of Belmont Music Publishers, Los Angeles, California 90049.

Example 67
BARTOK
Ten Easy Pieces
"Bear Dance"
(m. 18-28)

Example 68
TCHEREPNIN
Bagatelles Op. 5, # 6
(m. 11-13)

Examples of Changing Meters

Adler, Samuel   *Gradus I*, #7
Adler, Samuel   *Gradus I*, #8
Adler, Samuel   *Gradus I*, #9
Adler, Samuel   *Gradus I*, #15
Adler, Samuel   *Gradus I*, #16
°Adler, Samuel   *Gradus I*, #17
Adler, Samuel   *Gradus I*, #18
Adler, Samuel   *Gradus I*, #20
Bartok, Bela   *For Children, Vol. I*, #26
Bartok, Bela   *For Children, Vol. I*, #30
Diamond, David   *Album for the Young*, VIII ("The Sad Slant-Eyed Boy")
Finney, Ross Lee   *24 Piano Inventions*, #18 ("Walking")

INTERMEDIATE

Adler, Samuel   *Gradus II*, #7
Adler, Samuel   *Gradus II*, #10
Adler, Samuel   *Gradus II*, #18
Adler, Samuel   *Gradus II*, #20
American Music by Distinguished Composers, Book 2, "Perky Pete" by Leo Kraft
Bartok, Bela   *Mikrokosmos, Vol. IV*, #100
°Bartok, Bela   *Mikrokosmos, Vol. V*, #126 ("Change of Time")
Bartok, Bela   *Roumanian Folk Dances*, #5
°Bartok, Bela   *Ten Easy Pieces*, "Bear Dance" (see Example 67)
Contemporary Collection, Revised Edition, "Rain" by Dennis Riley
Fuleihan, Anis   *Ionian Pentagon*, #1
Fuleihan, Anis   *Ionian Pentagon*, #3
Fuleihan, Anis   *Ionian Pentagon*, #5
Hindemith, Paul   *Easy Five-Tone Pieces*, #9
Hindemith, Paul   *Easy Five-Tone Pieces*, #10
Kubik, Gail   *Sonatina for Piano*, First, Second and Fourth Movements
Masters of Our Day,   "The Young Pioneers" by Aaron Copland
Pinto, Octavio   *Scenas Infantis*, #4 ("Sleeping Time")
Pinto, Octavio   *Scenas Infantis*, #5 ("Hobby Horse")
Schuman, William   *Three Piano Moods*
Scriabin, Alexander   *Twenty-four Preludes*, #21
Starer, Robert   *Seven Vignettes*, VII ("Toccata")
Studies in 20th Century Idioms, "Variation on a Folk Song" by Keith Bissell

ADVANCED

Barber, Samuel   *Excursions Op. 20*, #1
Bartok, Bela   *Mikrokosmos, Vol. VI*, #140
Bartok, Bela   *Mikrokosmos, Vol. VI*, #141
Bernstein, Leonard   *Four Anniversaries*, "For David Diamond"
Britten, Benjamin   *Night-Piece*
Dello Joio, Norman   *Prelude: To a Young Musician*
Dello Joio, Norman   *Suite for Piano*, First, Second and Fourth Movements
Horizons, Book 2, "Scherzo" by Gerhard Wuensch
Ireland, John   *Sonatina*
Kabalevsky, Dmitri   *24 Preludes Op. 38*, #19
Kabalevsky, Dmitri   *24 Preludes Op. 38*, #20
Milano, Robert   *Toccata*
New Music for the Piano, "Capriccio" by Samuel Adler
New Music for the Piano, "Two Preludes," #2 by Kent Kennan
Poulenc, Francis   *Mouvements Perpetuels*, #3
Shostakovitch, Dmitri   *24 Preludes Op. 34*, #12
Shostakovitch, Dmitri   *24 Preludes Op. 34*, #13
Shostakovitch, Dmitri   *24 Preludes Op. 34*, #17

DIFFICULT

Barber, Samuel   *Nocturne*

INTERMEDIATE

Mompou, Frederic *Scènes d'Enfants*
°Stravinsky, Soulima *Six Sonatinas,* "Sonatina Prima," Third
   Movement (see Example 65)

ADVANCED

Harris, Roy *Piano Suite,* "Occupation"
New Music for the Piano, "Allegro Giocoso" by Leo Kraft
New Music for the Piano, "Piano Suite No. 3," Second Movement, by
   Miriam Gideon
New Music for the Piano, "Six Preludes Op. 20B" by George Perle
Stevens, Halsey *Seventeen Piano Pieces,* "Erratic Rhythms"
Stevens, Halsey *Seventeen Piano Pieces,* "Finale"

ELEMENTARY

Bartok, Bela *Mikrokosmos, Vol. II,* #60 (1/2)

INTERMEDIATE

Hindemith, Paul *Easy Five-Tone Pieces,* #10 (1/4)
°Tcherepnin, Alexander *Bagatelles Op. 5,* #6 (3/1 with dotted lines)
   (see Example 68)

ADVANCED

Bartok, Bela *Improvisations Op. 20,* #7 (2/4; 1/16)
Bartok, Bela *Mikrokosmos, Vol. VI,* #143 (1/4)
Britten, Benjamin *Night-Piece* (1/2)
Chavez, Carlos *Ten Preludes,* #8 (1/2)
°Schoenberg, Arnold *Suite für Klavier Op. 25,* "Praeludium" (see
   Example 66)

Excerpt from #17 from *Gradus I* by SAMUEL ADLER. Copyright 1971 by Oxford University Press, Inc. Reprinted by Permission.

Example 69
ADLER
Gradus I, #17
(m. 1-6)

Excerpt from *Mikrokosmos, Vol. V* by BELA BARTOK. Copyright 1940 by Hawkes & Son (London) Ltd., Renewed 1967. Reprinted by permission of Boosey & Hawkes, Inc.

Example 70
BARTOK
Mikrokosmos, Vol. V,
 #126
("Change of Time")
(m. 1-6)

Another metric innovation consists of *alternating two meters* throughout a work. This seems to be a substitute for longer asymmetric meters or asymmetric divisions which would otherwise result. For instance,

6/8 5/8 ♪♫♩.♫ | ♪♫♩.♫ instead of 11/8 ♪♫♩.♫ ♪♩.♫ ;

5/8 4/8 instead of $\frac{5+4}{8}$ ♩.♫♫♫♫♫

(9/8 would have three pulses per measure ♩.♫♫ ♪♫♫ ♫♫♩);

3/8 4/8 instead of 7/8, etc.

Both meter signatures are usually placed side by side at the beginning.

Examples of Alternating Meters

INTERMEDIATE
°Adler, Samuel   *Gradus II*, #2 (3/4 2/4)
Bartok, Bela   *Mikrokosmos, Vol. V*, #133 (5/4 4/4)
°Bartok, Bela   *Three Hungarian Folk-Tunes*, #2 (3/4 2/4)
°Bloch, Ernest   *Enfantines*, #5 ("Joyous March") (4/4 3/4)
Contemporary Collection, Revised Edition, "Lyric Piece" by Robert Lombardo (4/8 3/8)

ADVANCED
Scriabin, Alexander   *Twenty-four Preludes*, #16 (5/8 4/8)
Scriabin, Alexander   *Twenty-four Preludes*, #24 (6/8 5/8)
Stevens, Halsey   *Seventeen Piano Pieces*, "Study in Hemiola" (6/8 3/4)

Song-like ♩=132 (but each measure must be very free and loose)

Example 71
ADLER
Gradus II, #2
(m. 1-7)

Excerpt from #2 from *Gradus II* by SAMUEL ADLER. ° Copyright 1971, Oxford University Press, Inc. Reprinted by Permission.

Allegro non troppo, un poco rubato, ♩=ca 92

Example 72
BARTOK
Three Hungarian Folk-Tunes, #2
(m. 1-6)

Excerpt from *Three Hungarian Folk-Tunes* by BELA BARTOK. Reprinted from *Homage to Paderewski*. ° Copyright 1942 by Boosey & Hawkes, Inc. Reprinted by Permission.

Allegro giocoso(♩=132) (or 4/2 4/2)

Example 73
BLOCH
Enfantines, #5
("Joyous March")
(m. 1-4)

Excerpt from "Joyous March" from *Enfantines* by ERNEST BLOCH. ° Copyright MCMXXIV by Carl Fischer, Inc., New York. International Copyright Secured. Used by Permission.

Interest in the prose style of ancient plainchant was a primary factor in leading twentieth century composers to employ non-accented, speech rhythms; that is, rhythmic patterns whose formation has *not* been determined and limited by an inflexible metric accent. This kind of writing is characterized by ties over barlines, significant phrase markings and accents that are achieved by such means as duration and leaps. Changing meters have been particularly conducive to this free-flowing rhythm. Some composers have even resorted to omitting barlines altogether, as though they wanted to remove all chance of an undesirable downbeat accent by the performer.

INTERMEDIATE

°*American Composers of Today*, "Pastorale" from *Little Suite for Piano* by Lou Harrison

Diamond, David   *Alone at the Piano, Book 2*, #3

Diamond, David   *Alone at the Piano, Book 2*, #10

Finney, Ross Lee   *32 Piano Games*, XXVIII ("Mountains")

Finney, Ross Lee   *32 Piano Games*, XXIX ("Windows")

Finney, Ross Lee   *32 Piano Games*, XXX ("Mobile")

Finney, Ross Lee   *32 Piano Games*, XXXII ("Winter")

Ginastera, Alberto   *12 American Preludes, Vol. I*, #5 ("In the first Pentatonic Minor Mode")

Harris, Roy   *Little Suite*, "Bells"

°Hopkins, Antony   *Sonatine*, Second Movement

Horizons, Book 1, "Elegy for a Misty Afternoon" by Brian Cherney

Horizons, Book 2, "Wind-Harp" by John Beckwith

Masters of Our Day, "Song After Sundown" by Randall Thompson

°Persichetti, Vincent   *Little Piano Book*, #6 ("Arietta")

Schuman, William   *Three Piano Moods*, "Lyrical" (right hand)

°Stravinsky, Soulima   *Six Sonatinas*, "Sonatina Quarta" ("Plainchant"), Second Movement (see Example 40)

Examples of Prose Rhythms

Excerpt from *Little Suite for Piano* by LOU HARRISON. Reprinted from *American Composers of Today*. ° Copyright MCMLVI by Edward B. Marks Music Corporation. All Rights Reserved. International Copyright Secured. Used by Permission.

Example 74
HARRISON
Little Suite for Piano
"Pastorale"
(second score)

Excerpt from *Sonatine* by ANTONY HOPKINS. ° Copyright 1971 by Oxford University Press, Inc. Reprinted by Permission.

Example 75
HOPKINS
Sonatine
Second Movement
(first two scores)

Example 76
PERSICHETTI
Little Piano Book, #6
("Arietta")
(first score)

Polymeters

The simultaneous use of more than one rhythmic pattern, referred to as either *polymeter* or *polyrhythm*, constitutes one of the most daring steps toward the emancipation of rhythm in the twentieth century. This linear independence of rhythm, idiomatic in jazz improvisations, is similar to the melodic independence characteristic of dissonant counterpoint (see Chapter 5 on *Texture*). It is an outgrowth of such "cross rhythms" as two-against-three and three-against-four employed by nineteenth century composers.

Polymeters occur less frequently in piano music than in orchestral scores because of the obvious difficulties confronting a solo performer. This is especially true of very complex textures where barlines do not coincide every measure and the rhythmic phrases are of different lengths, as in the next example.

Example 77
BARTOK
String Quartet No. 2
Op. 17
First Movement
(m. 53-59)

Due to the fact that examples cited are selected primarily from intermediate-level piano literature, the reader will observe that there is only a suggestion of polymeter in some passages. An out-of-phase pattern or eighth notes beamed irregularly over barlines combined with another part which agrees with the prevailing meter can produce this effect.

ELEMENTARY

Adler, Samuel   *Gradus I,* #13

°*Contemporary Piano Literature, Book 2,* "Chimes" by Alexander Tcherepnin (out-of-phase pattern in right hand)

Stravinsky, Igor   *Les Cinq Doigts (The Five Fingers),* #2 (out-of-phase repeated patterns and irregularly beamed eighth notes)

Stravinsky, Igor   *Les Cinq Doigts (The Five Fingers),* #3 (irregularly beamed eighth notes)

INTERMEDIATE

°Bartok, Bela   *Mikrokosmos, Vol. V,* #125 ("Boating") (left hand pattern suggests 6/8 while right melody is in 3/4)(see Example 82)

°Bartok, Bela   *Mikrokosmos, Vol. V,* #138 ("Bagpipe") (left hand repeats a three-beat ostinato-pedal figure in 2/4)(see Example 88)

Contemporary Piano Literature, Book 4, "Merry-Go-Round" by Alexander Tcherepnin (right hand sounds a large 3/4 comprising two measures)

Gershwin, George   *Preludes for Piano,* II

Ginastera, Alberto   *12 American Preludes, Vol. I,* #1 ("Accents") (m. 10-13)

Ginastera, Alberto   *12 American Preludes, Vol. I,* #3 ("Creole Dance") (m. 9-12)

°Hindemith, Paul   *Easy Five-Tone Pieces,* #3 (two-and-one-half-beat left hand ostinato in 3/2)

Horizons, Book 1, "Toccatina" by M. Adaskin

Khachaturian, Aram   *Adventures of Ivan,* #4 ("Ivan Goes to a Party") (m. 37-42, two-beat left hand pattern in 3/4)

°Siegmeister, Elie   *American Kaleidoscope,* "Bicycle Wheels" (one-and-one-half beat repeated pattern in **C**)

Studies in 20th Century Idioms, "Six Little Etudes," #1 by Gerhard Wuensch

Studies in 20th Century Idioms, "Two in One" from *Intervals, Patterns, Shapes* by Brian Cherney

Tcherepnin, Alexander   *Bagatelles Op. 5,* #7

ADVANCED

Barber, Samuel   *Excursions Op. 20,* #4 (m. 38-39)

Bartok, Bela   *Mikrokosmos, Vol. VI,* #142 (m. 72-75)

Copland, Aaron   *The Cat and the Mouse* (m. 52-54)

Creston, Paul   *Six Preludes Op. 38,* #1

Creston, Paul   *Six Preludes Op. 38,* #3

Francaix, Jean   *Scherzo* (three-beat left hand pattern in 2/4)

Fuleihan, Anis   *Sonatina No. 2,* Second Movement (two-beat right hand pattern in 3/8)

Prokofiev, Serge   *Visions Fugitives Op. 22,* #15 (out-of-phase ostinato)

Prokofiev, Serge   *Visions Fugitives Op. 22,* #20 (first eight measures are written as 9/8 in right hand and 3/4 in left hand)

DIFFICULT

Mennin, Peter   *Five Piano Pieces,* "Variation-Canzona" (irregular beaming of eighths and sixteenths throughout)

Example 78
TCHEREPNIN
Chimes
(m. 17-20)

Example 79
HINDEMITH
Easy Five-Tone Pieces,
#3
(m. 1-2)

Example 80
SIEGMEISTER
American Kaleidoscope
"Bicycle Wheels"
(m. 1-2)

Ostinato and Pedal Point

The term *ostinato* means "obstinate" and refers to a recurring, short rhythmic pattern in the bass. Its forerunner is the *ground bass* or *cantus firmus* employed as a unifying agent in such eighteenth century variation forms as the *passacaglia*, where it is a recurring *melodic* pattern in the bass, and the *chaconne*, where a *harmonic* progression continually repeats. Unlike its predecessors, the ostinato is simply an accompaniment figure without the restriction of being associated with a variation form. It may be melodic or harmonic but not without strong rhythmic implications.

Example 81
PERSICHETTI
Parades for Piano
"March"
(m. 1-7)

When its length does not coincide with the confines or normal divisions of a measure, its rhythmic function is accentuated. The left hand ostinato in Example 82 actually sounds as 6/8.

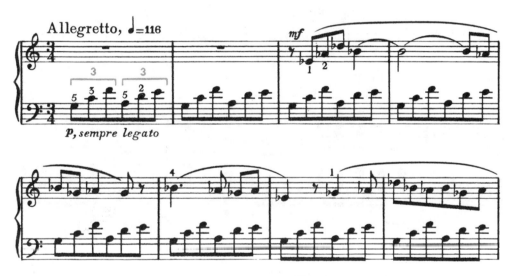

Example 82
BARTOK
Mikrokosmos, Vol. V,
#125
("Boating")
(m. 1-8)

Pedal point (also called *organ point*), a sustained bass tone over which harmonies change, was a common device in eighteenth century organ music in which its appearance on the dominant or tonic signaled the approaching conclusion of the piece. (An *inverted pedal point* occurs when the sustained tone is in an upper part.) Isolated examples of pedal point may be found in piano literature, but unless the bass tone is reiterated every measure or two, it becomes inaudible and, therefore, loses its rhythmic and harmonic effectiveness. In the following examples, compare the sustained cadential pedal points in Bach's *Fugue No. 1* and *Prelude No. 22* from the *Well-Tempered Clavier, Vol. I* with that of Chopin's *Prelude Op. 28 No. 17* where the tone is repeated intermittently for several pages.

Example 83
BACH, J. S.
Well-Tempered Clavier, Vol. I
"Fugue No. 1 in C"
(m. 23-27)

Example 84
BACH, J. S.
Well-Tempered Clavier, Vol. 1
"Prelude No. 22 in B♭ Minor"
(m. 1-2)

Example 85
CHOPIN
Prelude Op. 28 No. 17
(m. 75-85)

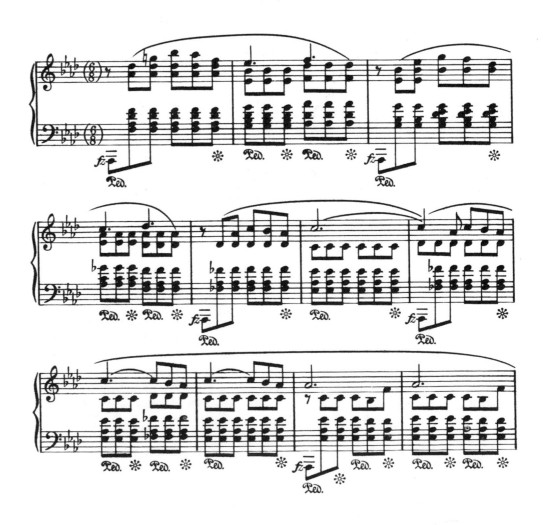

Impressionistic composers found both the pedal point and unobtrusive ostinato to be effective in establishing a floating or static condition necessary to the portrayal of light and color.

Example 86
GRIFFES
Three Tone-Pictures
"The Lake at Evening"
(m. 1-11)

Excerpt from *Three Tone-Pictures* by CHARLES GRIFFES. Copyright by G. Schirmer, Inc. Used by Permission.

Except in a gentle context, the pedal point in contemporary music takes on a vigorous role of frequent and sometimes brutal repetition. When it assumes such a rhythmic and dynamic character, its distinction from an ostinato becomes vague and pedantic. Bartok and Stravinsky exploited their capacities to generate a relentless energy. Other composers have taken a middle-of-the-road position.

Recent piano music abounds with pedal points and ostinatos, particularly the latter, and once they are identified, sightreading and memorizing are greatly facilitated.

Examples of Ostinato

ELEMENTARY

Adler, Samuel   *Gradus I,* #14
Contemporary Collection, Revised Edition, "Dusk" by Stanley Fletcher
Contemporary Collection, Revised Edition, "Intermezzo" by Frederick Koch
Contemporary Collection, Revised Edition, "Sitting Beside a River" by Avarham Sternklar
Contemporary Collection, Revised Edition, "Toccata Breve" by David Kraehenbuehl
Dello Joio, Norman   *Suite for the Young,* #8 ("A Sad Tale")
°Hindemith, Paul   *Easy Five-Tone Pieces,* #3 (see Example 79)
Kraehenbuehl, David   *Calendar Scenes,* #9 ("Labor Day Parade")
°Persichetti, Vincent   *Parades for Piano,* "March" (see Example 81)

Rollino, J., and Sheftel, P. *Festivities*, "Chinese Lanterns"
Rollino, J., and Sheftel, P. *Festivities*, "Hold Your Own"
Rollino, J., and Sheftel, P. *Festivities*, "Mixed Up March"
Rollino, J., and Sheftel, P. *Festivities*, "Yoghurt"
Stravinsky, Igor *Les Cinq Doigts (The Five Fingers)*, #2
Stravinsky, Igor *Les Cinq Doigts (The Five Fingers)*, #3
Stravinsky, Igor *Les Cinq Doigts (The Five Fingers)*, #5
Stravinsky, Igor *Les Cinq Doigts (The Five Fingers)*, #7
Stravinsky, Soulima *Piano Music for Children, Vol. I*, #4 ("Daddy is home")
Stravinsky, Soulima *Piano Music for Children, Vol. I*, #9 ("Pals")
Stravinsky, Soulima *Piano Music for Children, Vol. I*, #14 ("Pagoda")
Stravinsky, Soulima *Piano Music for Children, Vol. II*, #30 ("Iron Horse")

INTERMEDIATE

°Adler, Samual *Gradus II*, #1
Bartok, Bela *Fourteen Bagatelles Op. 6*, #2 (or advanced level)
Bartok, Bela *Fourteen Bagatelles Op. 6*, #5 (or advanced level)
Bartok, Bela *Mikrokosmos, Vol. III*, #47
Bartok, Bela *Mikrokosmos, Vol. III*, #48
Bartok, Bela *Mikrokosmos, Vol. IV*, #113
Bartok, Bela *Mikrokosmos, Vol. IV*, Appendix #33
°Bartok, Bela *Mikrokosmos, Vol. V*, #125 ("Boating") (see Example 82)
°Bartok, Bela *Mikrokosmos, Vol. V*, #138 ("Bagpipe")
°Casella, Alfredo *11 Children's Pieces*, I ("Preludio")
°Casella, Alfredo *11 Children's Pieces*, IV ("Bolero") (see Example 38)
°Casella, Alfredo *11 Children's Pieces*, IX ("Carillon") (see Example 179)
Casella, Alfredo *11 Children's Pieces*, X ("Berceuse")
Contemporary Collection, Revised Edition, "Evening Song" by Gerald Shapiro
Contemporary Piano Literature, Book 5-6, "Night" by Ross Lee Finney
Contemporary Piano Literature, Book 5-6, "Song" by Ross Lee Finney
Creston, Paul *Five Little Dances*, "Rustic Dance"
Dello Joio, Norman *Lyric Pieces for the Young*, #1 ("Boat Song")
Dello Joio, Norman *Lyric Pieces for the Young*, #4 ("Night Song")
Finney, Ross Lee *24 Piano Inventions*, #21 ("Twilight")
Finney, Ross Lee *24 Piano Inventions*, #22 ("A Sad Song")
Fletcher, Stanley *Street Scenes*, "Night Patrol"
Fletcher, Stanley *Street Scenes*, "Parade Around the Block"
Goossens, Eugene *Kaleidoscope*, "A Ghost Story"
Goossens, Eugene *Kaleidoscope*, "The Hurdy-Gurdy Man"
Goossens, Eugene *Kaleidoscope*, "The Old Musical-Box"
Goossens, Eugene *Kaleidoscope*, "Promenade"
Goossens, Eugene *Kaleidoscope*, "The Rocking-Horse"
Masters of Our Day, "Touches Blanches" by Darius Milhaud
Mompou, Frederic *Scènes d'Enfants*, "Cris dans la Rue"
Prokofiev, Serge *Children's Pieces Op. 65*, #3 ("A Little Story")
Rebikov, Vladimir *Silhouettes*, "Strolling Musicians"
Schuman, William *Three Piano Moods*, "Lyrical"
Shostakovitch, Dmitri *Dances of the Dolls*, #6 ("Hurdy-Gurdy")
Siegmeister, Elie *American Kaleidoscope*, "March"
Siegmeister, Elie *American Kaleidoscope*, "The Toy Railroad"
Starer, Robert *Seven Vignettes*, VI ("The Camel and the Moon") (see Example 159)
Stravinsky, Soulima *Six Sonatinas*, "Sonatina Quarta"
Studies in 20th Century Idioms, "Ostinette" by F.R.C. Clarke
Tansman, Alexandre *Pour les Enfants, 4th Set*, #4 ("Cache-Cache")
Tansman, Alexandre *Pour les Enfants, 4th Set*, #5 ("In a Venetian Gondola")

Tansman, Alexandre *Pour les Enfants, 4th Set,* #9 ("Berceuse")
Tansman, Alexandre *Pour les Enfants, 4th Set,* #10 ("Marche Militaire")
Tcherepnin, Alexander *Bagatelles Op. 5,* #4
Toch, Ernst *Echoes from a Small Town Op. 49,* #2
Toch, Ernst *Echoes from a Small Town Op. 49,* #6
Toch, Ernst *Echoes from a Small Town Op. 49,* #9
Toch, Ernst *Echoes from a Small Town Op. 49,* #11
Toch, Ernst *Echoes from a Small Town Op. 49,* #12
Toch, Ernst *Echoes from a Small Town Op. 49,* #14

ADVANCED

Barber, Samuel *Excursions Op. 20,* #1
Barber, Samuel *Excursions Op. 20,* #3
°Bartok, Bela *Mikrokosmos, Vol. VI,* #146 ("Ostinato")
Bartok, Bela *Mikrokosmos, Vol. VI,* #147
Bartok, Bela *Mikrokosmos, Vol. VI,* #153
Bartok, Bela *Suite Op. 14,* #2
Britten, Benjamin *Night-Music*
Creston, Paul *Six Preludes Op. 38,* #2
Creston, Paul *Six Preludes Op. 38,* #4
Kabalevsky, Dmitri *24 Preludes Op. 38,* #4
Lloyd, Norman *Episodes for Piano*
Milhaud, Darius *Saudades do Brazil, Book 2,* #7 ("Corcovado")
Milhaud, Darius *Saudades do Brazil, Book 2,* #9 ("Sumaré")
Poulenc, Francis *Mouvements Perpetuels,* #1
Prokofiev, Serge *Visions Fugitives Op. 22,* #3
Prokofiev, Serge *Visions Fugitives Op. 22,* #10
Prokofiev, Serge *Visions Fugitives Op. 22,* #11
Prokofiev, Serge *Visions Fugitives Op. 22,* #15
Szmanowski, Karol *Mazurkas Op. 50, Book 1,* #2

DIFFICULT

Palmer, Robert *Toccata Ostinato*
Prokofiev, Serge *Four Pieces Op. 4,* "Despair"

Example 87
ADLER
Gradus II, #1
(m. 1-10)

Excerpt from #1 from *Gradus II* by SAMUEL ADLER. ᶜ Copyright 1971 by Oxford University Press, Inc. Reprinted by Permission.

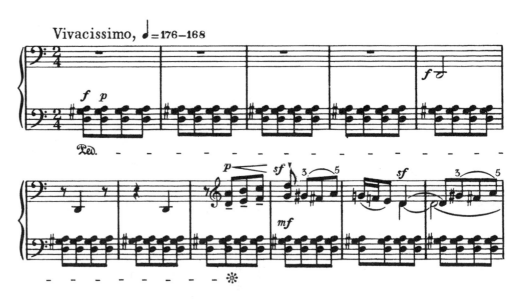

ELEMENTARY

    Contemporary Collection, Revised Edition, "Between Sleep and Waking" by Stanley Fletcher

    Stravinsky, Igor   *Les Cinq Doigts (The Five Fingers)*, #4 (inverted pedal point)

INTERMEDIATE

    Adler, Samuel   *Gradus II*, #2

    American Composers of Today, "Lullaby" by Alan Hovhaness

    Bartok, Bela   *For Children, Vol. I*, #27

    Bartok, Bela   *For Children, Vol. I*, #30

    Bartok, Bela   *For Children, Vol. I*, #40

    Bartok, Bela   *For Children, Vol. II*, #30

    Bartok, Bela   *Mikrokosmos, Vol. IV*, #107

    Bartok, Bela   *Roumanian Folk Dances*, #3

    Bartok, Bela   *Roumanian Folk Dances*, #4

    Bartok, Bela   *Roumanian Folk Dances*, #5

    Bartok, Bela   *Roumanian Folk Dances*, #6

    Bartok, Bela   *Sonatina*, First and Third Movements

    Casella, Alfredo   *11 Children's Pieces*, VI ("Siciliana")

    °Casella, Alfredo   *11 Children's Pieces*, VIII ("Minuetto")

    Contemporary Collection, Revised Edition, "Etude in Blue" by David Kraehenbuehl

    Creston, Paul   *Five Little Dances*, "Pastoral Dance"

    °Creston, Paul   *Five Little Dances*, "Toy Dance"

    Ginastera, Alberto   *12 American Preludes, Vol. II*, #12 ("In the first Pentatonic Major Mode")

    Hindemith, Paul   *Easy Five-Tone Pieces*, #8

    Hindemith, Paul   *Easy Five-Tone Pieces*, #9

    Khachaturian, Aram   *Adventures of Ivan*, #3 ("Ivan is Ill")

    Khachaturian, Aram   *Adventures of Ivan*, #13 ("Ivan is Very Busy")

    Mompou, Frederic   *Scènes d'Enfants*, "Jeu"

    Pinto, Octavio   *Scenas Infantis*, #2 ("Ring Around the Rosy")

    Pinto, Octavio   *Scenas Infantis*, #3 ("March Little Soldier")

    Pinto, Octavio   *Scenas Infantis*, #4 ("Sleeping Time")

    Pinto, Octavio   *Scenas Infantis*, #5 ("Hobby Horse")

    Prokofiev, Serge   *Children's Pieces Op. 65*, #1 ("Morning")

    Prokofiev, Serge   *Children's Pieces Op. 65*, #11 ("Evening")

    Prokofiev, Serge   *Children's Pieces Op. 65*, #12 ("The Moon Strolls in the Meadows")

    Rebikov, Vladimir   *Silhouettes*, "The Lame Witch Lurking in the Forest"

    Rebikov, Vladimir   *Silhouettes*, "Little Girl Rocking Her Dolly"

ADVANCED

    Bartok, Bela   *Three Rondos*, II

    °Griffes, Charles   *Three Tone-Pictures*, "The Lake at Evening" (see Example 86)

    Kabalevsky, Dmitri   *24 Preludes Op. 38*, #13 (pedal point covers four-octave span)

    Piston, Walter   *Passacaglia* (inverted pedal at beginning and end)

    Prokofiev, Serge   *Visions Fugitives Op. 22*, #16

    Villa-Lobos, Heitor   *The Three Maries*, "Alnilam"

Example 91
CASELLA
11 Children's Pieces, VIII
("Minuetto")
(m. 37-47)

Excerpt from *11 Children's Pieces* by ALFREDO CASELLA. ' Copyright 1921 by Universal Edition A.G., Wien, Renewed 1949. Used by Permission of Universal Edition A.G.

Example 92
CRESTON
Five Little Dances
"Toy Dance"
(m. 1-8)

Excerpt from *Five Little Dances* by PAUL CRESTON. Copyright by G. Schirmer, Inc. Used by Permission.

Pulsating Rhythm

The driving energy of the machine-age is reflected in this next device, *pulsating rhythm*. Repeated-note ostinatos with relentless regularity is the common means used by Bartok, Prokofiev, Shostakovitch and Stravinsky for creating this effect. When the repeated pattern is dissonant, its brutal force is increased. Such strident sound is one of Stravinsky's trademarks.

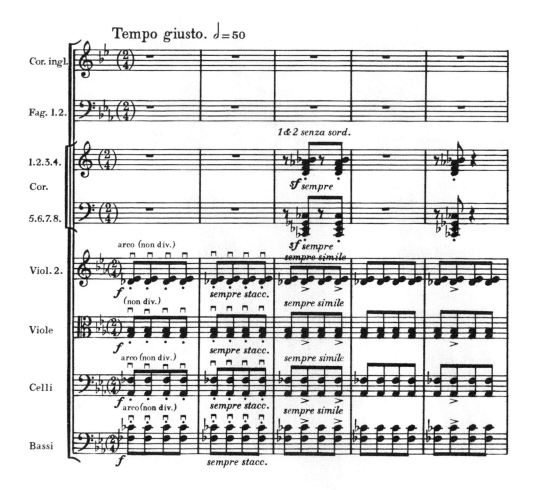

Example 93
STRAVINSKY
The Rite of Spring
"Danses des
Adolescentes"
(m. 1-9)

Excerpt from *The Rite of Spring* by IGOR STRAVINSKY from the Kalmus score. Used by Permission of Edwin F. Kalmus

Examples of Pulsating Rhythm

Example 94
BARTOK
For Children, Vol. I, #6
(m. 1-14)

Excerpt from *For Children, Vol. I* by BELA BARTOK. Reprinted from *Bela Bartok: An Introduction to the Composer and his Music.* Copyright 1975 by General Words and Music Company. Reprinted by Permission.

Example 95
BARTOK
Fourteen Bagatelles
Op. 6, #2
(m. 1-6)

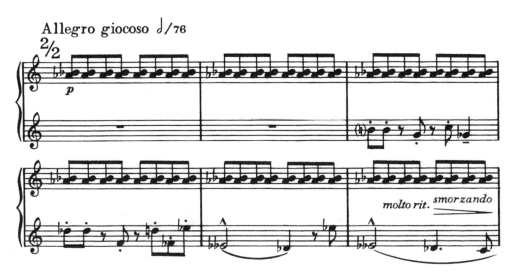

Excerpt from *Fourteen Bagatelles Op. 6* by BELA BARTOK. Used by Permission of Edwin F. Kalmus.

Allegro vivace ♩=104–120

Example 96
BARTOK
Ten Easy Pieces
"Bear Dance"
(m. 1-11)

Excerpt from *Ten Easy Pieces* by BELA BARTOK. Used by permission of Edwin F. Kalmus.

Example 97
DELLO JOIO
Lyric Pieces for the Young,
 # 6
("Russian Dancer")
(m. 21-24)

Excerpt from *Lyric Pieces for the Young* by NORMAN DELLO JOIO. ⁶ Copyright MCMLXXI by Edward B. Marks Music Corporation. All Rights Reserved. International Copyright Secured. Used by Permission.

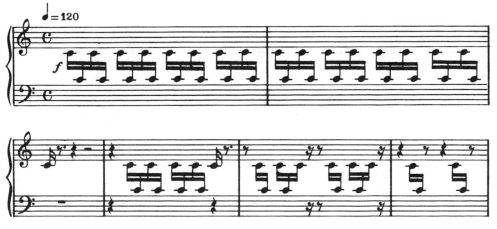

Example 98
FINNEY
32 Piano Games, XX
("Argument")
(m. 1-6)

Excerpt from *32 Piano Games* by ROSS LEE FINNEY (P 66256). ⁶ Copyright 1969 by Henmar Press, Inc., 373 Park Avenue South, New York, New York 10016. Reprint permission granted by the publisher.

Suggested Assignments

1. Play and study a representative sampling of the piano pieces listed.

2. For additional resource reading, see the following:

   Creston   *Principles of Rhythm*
   Dallin   *Techniques of Twentieth Century Composition*, Chapters 5 and 11.

3. Listen to the following complete works, with score if possible:

   Bartok   *Piano Concerto No. 3* (especially the Second Movement for simple rhythm)
   Bartok   *String Quartet No. 2*, Second Movement (pulsating rhythm)
   Bartok   *String Quartet No. 4*, Fifth Movement (ostinato, pedal point, pulsating rhythm, mirror, inversion, canon)
   Bartok   *Mikrokosmos, Vol. VI,* #148-153, "Six Dances in Bulgarian Rhythm" (meters)
   Bernstein   *Chichester Psalms* (7/8 and 10/4 in First and Third Movements, respectively)
   Carter   *String Quartet No. 2* (rhythmic effects including polyrhythms)
   Creston   *Symphony No. 1* (especially the rhythmic Second Movement)
   Creston   *Symphony No. 3* (Gregorian themes throughout)
   Hanson   *Symphony No. 1* ("Nordic"), First Movement (5/4)
   Hindemith   *String Quartet Op. 22*, Second Movement (changing meters, though none are written in)
   Prokofiev   *Suggestion Diabolique Op. 4* for piano (percussive and pulsating)
   Shostakovitch   *Symphony No. 5* (Compare the rhythm of the Third and Fourth Movements.)
   Stravinsky   *L'Histoire du Soldat*, "The Soldier's March" (ostinato causing polymeters)
   Stravinsky   *Petrouchka* (changing and polymeters in first scene)
   Stravinsky   *The Rite of Spring* (numerous rhythmic devices throughout)
   Stravinsky   *Symphony of Psalms*, III (ostinato, especially page 35 to the end)
   Tchaikovsky   *Symphony No. 6*, Second Movement (5/4)
   Walton, William   *Belshazzer's Feast* (changing meters, ostinato, polymeters)

4. Write a two-part rhythm study using changing meters, including some asymmetric.

5. Using the following rhythmic motive in 8/8 time, compose a miniature piece for the instrument or ensemble of your choice: ♪♩ ♪♫ ♫

Chapter 3
Harmony

Careful analysis of any musical excerpt from the seventeenth, eighteenth or nineteenth centuries reveals that all chords were *tertian,* most of them contained three or four different tones and were called *triads* or *seventh* chords. During the first part of this period, tonality was firmly established at the outset of a work by melodic and harmonic emphasis upon the tonic chord and by frequent use of the primary triads I, IV and V. Secondary triads were used as substitutes for variety and color. The main function of chromatic chords was that of decoration or embellishment, similar to adjectives and adverbs in grammar.

However, during the nineteenth century, chromatic harmony increased in frequency and significance, resulting in longer time spans between simple progressions such as I-V, as well as between dissonant and/or chromatic chords and their resolutions. This often delayed the establishment of tonality, weakening it and leaving it vague in the listener's ear.

At the same time, the dominant ninth chord became popular among romantic composers who employed it either for its lush and pleasing sound or for its dramatic and climactic quality. By the turn-of-the-century (Impressionistic period), ninths and also elevenths and thirteenths appeared on chords other than the dominant. Such skyscraper-like chords contain most or all of the scale degrees, so passages consisting chiefly of these are thick and immobile. When all their chord members are present, resolution as such becomes impossible. Thus, harmony became *non-functional;* that is, chords were used primarily for their colorful effects. Instead of following prescribed rules of progression designed to lead back to the tonic, they behaved in new and unexpected ways. Successions of unrelated chords, parallelism, consonant use of previously considered dissonances, and chords with both major and minor thirds became normative.

As the twentieth century progressed, other harmonic procedures emerged, including polychords, non-tertian structures, serial chords, "wrong-note" writing, harmonics and percussive use of harmony. This is not to say that older styles were totally repudiated, for composers did not recklessly discard the technics of the past, but rather, increased their materials by building upon them. (At this point, the reader will find it beneficial to read Appendix B on *The Tonal Period and Its Gradual Breakdown*.)

Tertian:

Triads, Seventh and Ninth Chords

Though functional harmony has been almost completely abandoned by twentieth century composers, tertian chords have not. Drawing from an enlarged field of twelve tones (dodecuple scale), composers lavishly and freely employ triads, seventh, and ninth chords in successive or parallel diatonic and chromatic relationships. They are not chosen haphazardly, though it is true they do not always "match" whatever else is going on. Rather, they are selected discriminately for their colorful effects. Dissonant chords have been liberated from strict resolution formulas to parallel and free-floating behaviorisms. When surrounded by greater dissonance and activity they can even function as "tonics" or final points of repose.

Examples of Triads, Seventh and Ninth Chords

ELEMENTARY

Adler, Samuel *Gradus I*, #19
Adler, Samuel *Gradus I*, #20
Kabalevsky, Dmitri *24 Little Pieces for Children Op. 39*, #12
Kabalevsky, Dmitri *24 Little Pieces for Children Op. 39*, #18
Stravinsky, Soulima *Piano Music for Children, Vol. II*, #23 ("Cops and robbers")

INTERMEDIATE

Bartok, Bela *Fourteen Bagatelles Op. 6*, #5 (or advanced level)
Bartok, Bela *Fourteen Bagatelles Op. 6*, #13
Bartok, Bela *Fourteen Bagatelles Op. 6*, #14
°Bartok, Bela *Mikrokosmos, Vol. III*, #69 ("Chord Study")
Bartok, Bela *Mikrokosmos, Vol. III*, #73
Bartok, Bela *Mikrokosmos, Vol. III*, #85
Bartok, Bela *Mikrokosmos, Vol. IV*, #120
Bartok, Bela *Mikrokosmos, Vol. V*, #129
Bartok, Bela *Mikrokosmos, Vol. V*, #133
Bartok, Bela *Ten Easy Pieces*, "Bear Dance"
Casella, Alfredo *11 Children's Pieces*, VI ("Siciliana")
Contemporary Collection, Revised Edition, "Fanfares" by Gerald Shapiro
Contemporary Collection, Revised Edition, "Siciliana" by Robert Keys Clark
Contemporary Piano Literature, Book 5-6, "Happy Stowaway" by Alexander Tcherepnin
Contemporary Piano Literature, Book 5-6, "Vacation" by Ross Lee Finney
Creston, Paul *Five Little Dances*, "Languid Dance"
Dello Joio, Norman *Lyric Pieces for the Young*, #2 ("Prayer of the Matador")
°Finney, Ross Lee *24 Piano Inventions*, #23 ("Playing Ball")

Goossens, Eugene *Kaleidoscope*, "The Clockwork Dancer" (parallel V_7's)
Goossens, Eugene *Kaleidoscope*, "Good Morning"
Goossens, Eugene *Kaleidoscope*, "March of the Wooden Soldiers"
Goossens, Eugene *Kaleidoscope*, "A Merry Party"
Hopkins, Antony *Sonatine*, First and Third Movements
°Kabalevsky, Dmitri *Children's Pieces Op. 27*, "Fairy Tale"
Kabalevsky, Dmitri *Children's Pieces Op. 27*, "Toccatina"
Khachaturian, Aram *Adventures of Ivan*, #4 ("Ivan Goes to a Party") (parallel V_7's)
Kubik, Gail *Sonatina for Piano*, Second and Fourth Movements
Masters of Our Day, "Dance of the Warriors" by Howard Hanson
Mompou, Frederic *Scènes d'Enfants*, "Jeux sur la Place" (ninth chord as tonic)
Persichetti, Vincent *Little Piano Book*, #14 ("Gloria")
°Persichetti, Vincent *Piano Sonatina No. 4*, Third Movement
Pinto, Octavio *Scenas Infantis*, #1 ("Run, Run!")
Pinto, Octavio *Scenas Infantis*, #2 ("Ring Around the Rosy")
Prokofiev, Serge *Four Pieces Op. 32*, "Minuet"
Siegmeister, Elie *American Kaleidoscope*, "Street Games"
Starer, Robert *Sketches in Color*, #4 ("Bright Orange")

ADVANCED

Bartok, Bela *Mikrokosmos, Vol. VI*, #153
Bartok, Bela *Three Rondos*, I
Bartok, Bela *Three Rondos*, II
Copland, Aaron *The Cat and the Mouse*
Gershwin, George *Preludes for Piano*, I (parallel V_{13}'s)
Kabalevsky, Dmitri *24 Preludes Op. 38*, #4
Kabalevsky, Dmitri *24 Preludes Op. 38*, #23
Kabalevsky, Dmitri *24 Preludes Op. 38*, #24
Peeters, Flor *Toccata*
Prokofiev, Serge *Visions Fugitives Op. 22*, #1
Prokofiev, Serge *Visions Fugitives Op. 22*, #3
Prokofiev, Serge *Visions Fugitives Op. 22*, #15

Example 99
BARTOK
Mikrokosmos, Vol. III,
#69
("Chord Study")
(m. 1-7)

Example 100
FINNEY
24 Piano Inventions, #23
("Playing Ball")
(m. 1-9)

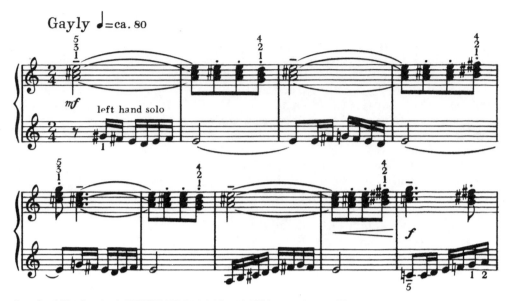

Gayly ♩=ca. 80

mf

left hand solo

Example 101
KABALEVSKY
Children's Pieces Op. 27
"Fairy Tale"
(m. 1-4)

Andantino cantabile

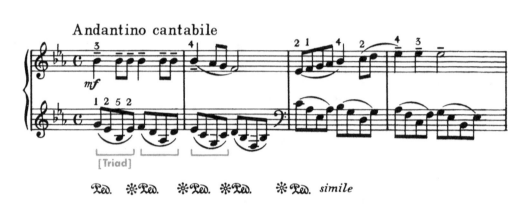

[Triad]

℘ed.   ℘ed.   ℘ed.   ℘ed.   ℘ed. *simile*

Example 102
PERSICHETTI
Piano Sonatina No. 4
Third Movement
(m. 1-12)

Moderato

mf dolce

[Seventh]

P_____ P_____ P simile

Equal treatment of all twelve tones led to the demise of the uniquely distinct major and minor modes. In their wake appeared the *major-minor* (or split third) chord, considered to be Igor Stravinsky's favorite, which contains both a major and a minor third. With the minor third on top, an octave or more usually separates the two tones which sometimes sound successively rather than simultaneously.

Tertian:
Major-Minor Chords

Example 103
Major-Minor Chords

Examples of Major-Minor Chords

ELEMENTARY
°Kabalevsky, Dmitri *24 Little Pieces for Children Op. 39,* #20
Stravinsky, Soulima *Piano Music for Children, Vol. I,* #12 ("Pastoral tune")

INTERMEDIATE
°Bartok, Bela *Mikrokosmos, Vol. V,* #125 ("Boating") (final chord)
Contemporary Collection, Revised Edition, "Procession" by Norman Auerbach
Goossens, Eugene *Kaleidoscope,* "Good Night" (m. 22)
°Hindemith, Paul *Easy Five-Tone Pieces,* #6

ADVANCED
Bartok, Bela *Mikrokosmos, Vol. VI,* #143
Bartok, Bela *Mikrokosmos, Vol. VI,* #151 (cadence in fast succession)
Bartok, Bela *Suite Op. 14*
Bartok, Bela *Three Rondos,* I
Gershwin, George *Preludes for Piano,* I
Hindemith, Paul *Ludus Tonalis,* "Fuga duodecima in F♯" (second theme)
°Milhaud, Darius *Saudades do Brazil, Book 2,* #8 ("Tijuca")
Shostakovitch, Dmitri *24 Preludes Op. 34,* #24
Villa-Lobos, Heitor *The Three Maries,* "Alnitah"

DIFFICULT
Ginastera, Alberto *12 American Preludes, Vol. I,* #2 ("Sadness") (cadence)

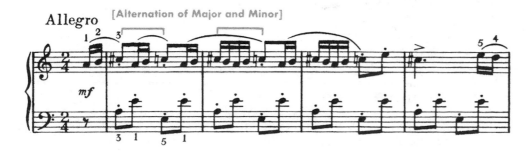

Example 104
KABALEVSKY
24 Little Pieces for Children Op. 39, #20
(m. 1-4)

Excerpt from *24 Little Pieces for Children Op. 39* by DMITRI KABALEVSKY. Reprinted from *Piano Literature, Vol. II.* ' Copyright 1966 by General Words and Music Company. Reprinted by Permission.

Example 105
BARTOK
Mikrokosmos, Vol. V,
#125
("Boating")
(m. 43-47)

Example 106
HINDEMITH
Easy Five-Tone Pieces, #6
(m. 11-14)

Example 107
MILHAUD
Saudades do Brazil,
Book 2, #8
("Tijuca")
(m. 48-52)

Non-Tertian:

Quartal, Quintal, Secundal (Clusters), $\frac{5}{4}$, Added Note and Complex Chords

As noted earlier in this chapter, tertian harmony not only survived the breakdown of the major-minor tonal system but grew in vitality and color in the hands of contemporary composers. Furthermore, harmonic intervals of fourths, fifths, seconds, sevenths and tritones were given consonant status, meaning they were stable and complete in themselves and did not need resolution. In addition, *non-tertian* sonorities, which were first created by delayed resolutions of suspensions in the nineteenth century (as at ° in the Chopin excerpt below), came into being as independent chords in the twentieth century.

Example 108
CHOPIN
Prelude Op. 28 No. 4
(m. 18-21)

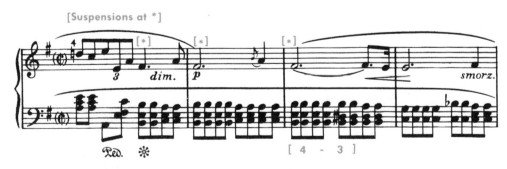

The four-three suspension produced the momentary sound of a chord built in fourths or fifths. As time progressed, *quartal, quintal* and $\frac{5}{4}$ *chords* evolved. The latter chord, used so much by Debussy, contains both the intervals of a fourth and a fifth.

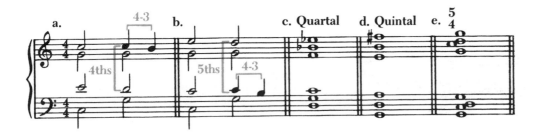

Example 109
**Quartal, Quintal and $\frac{5}{4}$
Chords**

Other non-tertian structures were formed by combining seconds together into *secundal* chords, known as *tone clusters,* and *adding notes* to already existing tertian chords. The added second and sixth are the most common.

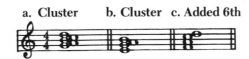

Example 110
Clusters and Added Notes

Up to twelve tones can be stacked on top of each other producing complex, sky-scraper-like structures with novel, kaleidoscopic color. Because of their un-wieldy size, they are uncommon in piano literature. However, in orchestral writing they are used for percussive effects of punctuation, as in Example 111, or in parallel motion.

Example 111
SCHULLER
*Seven Studies on Themes
of Paul Klee,* III
(**"Little Blue Devil"**)
(m. 76-79, partial score)

Examples of Quartal, Quintal, Secundal (Clusters), $\frac{5}{4}$, Added Note, and Complex Chords

ELEMENTARY

°Adler, Samuel   *Gradus I*, #16 (clusters)
Adventures in Time and Space, Vol. I, "Clouds" by Mary Mageau (clusters)
Contemporary Collection, Revised Edition, "Between Sleep and Waking" by Stanley Fletcher (clusters)
Dello Joio, Norman   *Suite for the Young*, #8 (sevenths; clusters)
Diamond, David   *Album for the Young*, III ("Happy-Go-Lucky") (fifths)
Diamond, David.   *Album for the Young*, IV ("Tender Thoughts") (fifths)
Diamond, David   *Album for the Young*, VI ("Christmastide") (many non-tertian)
Diamond, David   *Album for the Young*, VII ("Spring Song") (fifths)
Olson, Lynn Freeman   *Menagerie*, "The Grumpy Bear" (seconds)
Olson, Lynn Freeman   *Menagerie*, "The Prickly Porcupine" (seconds)
Siegmeister, Elie   *American Kaleidoscope*, "Banjo Tune" (added sixth)
Stravinsky, Soulima   *Piano Music for Children, Vol. I*, #14 ("Pagoda") (sevenths)

INTERMEDIATE

°Adler, Samuel   *Gradus II*, #3 (clusters)
°Adler, Samuel   *Gradus II*, #6 (clusters)
American Composers of Today, "March of the Puppets" by Sol Berkowitz
American Music by Distinguished Composers, "The Flickering Candle" by Bernard Wagenaar
American Music by Distinguished Composers, "Perky Pete" by Leo Kraft
American Music by Distinguished Composers, "Sway Dance" by Henry Cowell
Bartok, Bela   *Fourteen Bagatelles Op. 6*, #2 (or advanced level)
°Bartok, Bela   *Fourteen Bagatelles Op. 6*, #5 (added note) (or advanced level)
Bartok, Bela   *Fourteen Bagatelles Op. 6*, #6 (fifths)
°Bartok, Bela   *Fourteen Bagatelles Op. 6*, #11 (quartal chords doubling melody)
Bartok, Bela   *Mikrokosmos, Vol. III*, #89 ($\frac{5}{4}$)
Bartok, Bela   *Mikrokosmos, Vol. IV*, #107 (clusters)
Bartok, Bela   *Mikrokosmos, Vol. IV*, #115 ("Bulgarian Rhythm") (parallel sevenths)
Bartok, Bela   *Mikrokosmos, Vol. V*, #122 (clusters; $\frac{5}{4}$)
°Bartok, Bela   *Mikrokosmos, Vol. V*, #124 ("Staccato") (tritones)
°Bartok, Bela   *Mikrokosmos, Vol. V*, #130
Bartok, Bela   *Mikrokosmos, Vol. V*, #132
Bartok, Bela   *Mikrokosmos, Vol. V*, #133 (clusters; seconds; added note)
Bloch, Ernest   *Enfantines*, #9 ("Teasing") (clusters)
Casella, Alfredo   *11 Children's Pieces*, I ("Preludio") (fourths)
Casella, Alfredo   *11 Children's Pieces*, X ("Berceuse") (fifths)
Contemporary Collection, Revised Edition, "Dirge" by William Pottebaum (fourths; fifths)
Contemporary Collection, Revised Edition, "Rain" by Dennis Riley (seconds)
Contemporary Collection, Revised Edition, "Scherzo" by Dennis Riley (seconds)
Contemporary Collection, Revised Edition, "Three Short Pieces," I by Hugh Aitken (fifths)
Fennimore, Joseph   *Bits and Pieces*, "Dance of the Dinosaurs"

Finney, Ross Lee   *24 Piano Inventions,* #10 ("Playing Tag") (clusters; seconds)
°Finney, Ross Lee   *32 Piano Games,* XI ("3 White-Note Clusters, High and Low") (nearly all the pieces have clusters)
Finney, Ross Lee   *32 Piano Games,* XXVII ("Mirror Waltz") (seconds
Fletcher, Stanley   *Street Scenes,* "Barking Dog" (clusters)
Fletcher, Stanley   *Street Scenes,* "Parade Around the Block" (clusters)
Fletcher, Stanley   *Street Scenes,* "Sparrows" (seconds)
Fletcher, Stanley   *Street Scenes,* "Traffic Cop" (added note)
Ginastera, Alberto   *12 American Preludes, Vol. I,* #1 ("Accents") (broken quintal)
Goossens, Eugene   *Kaleidoscope,* "March of the Wooden Soldiers" (fourths; fifths; seventh chords)
Hindemith, Paul   *Easy Five-Tone Pieces,* #4 (seconds; fourths)
°Hindemith, Paul   *Easy Five-Tone Pieces,* #5 (added note)
Mompou, Frederic   *Scènes d'Enfants,* "Cris dans la Rue" (quartal)
Mompou, Frederic   *Scènes d'Enfants,* "Jeune Filles au Jardin" (fourths; quintal; added note)
Pentland, Barbara   *Space Studies,* II ("From Outer Space")
Pinto, Octavio   *Scenas Infantis,* #4 ("Sleeping Time") (added note chords doubling melody)
Prokofiev, Serge   *Children's Pieces Op. 65,* #8 ("The Rain and the Rainbow") (clusters)
°Starer, Robert   *Seven Vignettes,* II ("Song Without Words") (sevenths)
Starer, Robert   *Seven Vignettes,* VI ("The Camel and the Moon") (ostinato in seconds)
Starer, Robert   *Seven Vignettes,* VII ("Toccata") (tritone bass)
Studies in 20th Century Idioms, "Sonorous Seconds" from *Intervals, Patterns, Shapes* by Brian Cherney

ADVANCED
Bartok, Bela   *Mikrokosmos, Vol. VI,* #140
Bartok, Bela   *Mikrokosmos, Vol. VI,* #142
Bartok, Bela   *Mikrokosmos, Vol. VI,* #144 (seconds)
Bartok, Bela   *Suite Op. 14,* #2 (seconds)
Bartok, Bela   *Three Rondos,* II
Bartok, Bela   *Three Rondos,* III (added note; clusters)
°Bernstein, Leonard   *Four Anniversaries,* "For David Diamond" (quintal)
Bernstein, Leonard   *Four Anniversaries,* "For Johnny Mehegan" (quartal)
Cowell, Henry   *Piano Music,* "Exultation" (large clusters played by hand and forearm)
Cowell, Henry   *Piano Music,* "The Tides of Manaunaun" (large clusters played by hand and forearm)
Dello Joio, Norman   *Suite for Piano* (fourths; fifths; sevenths; quartal)
Francaix, Jean   *Scherzo* (quartal)
Harris, Roy   *Piano Suite,* "Contemplation" (quartal)
Harris, Roy   *Piano Suite,* "Occupation" (quartal)
Harris, Roy   *Piano Suite,* "Recreation" (clusters)
Harris, Roy   *Toccata* (fourths; fifths; added note)
Kennan, Kent   *Three Preludes,* #1 (added note)
Kennan, Kent   *Three Preludes,* #2 (quartal; quintal; added note)
Khachaturian, Aram   *Toccata* (broken quartal)
Lloyd, Norman   *Episodes for Piano,* #3 (clusters; added note)
Milano, Robert   *Toccata* (fourths; fifths; $\frac{5}{4}$)
Milhaud, Darius   *Saudades do Brazil, Book 2,* #7 ("Corcovado") (fourths)

Milhaud, Darius *Saudades do Brazil, Book 2*, #8 ("Tijuca") (seconds; parallel seventh chords)

Milhaud, Darius *Saudades do Brazil, Book 2*, #9 ("Sumaré") (quartal chords doubling melody)

New Music for the Piano, "Two Preludes," #2 by Kent Kennan (quartal)

Piston, Walter *Passacaglia* (quartal)

Prokofiev, Serge *Visions Fugitives Op. 22*, #3 (seconds)

Prokofiev, Serge *Visions Fugitives Op. 22*, #14 (clusters; seconds)

Prokofiev, Serge *Visions Fugitives Op. 22*, #20 (quartal)

Riegger, Wallingford *New and Old*, #10 ("Tone Clusters") (also quartal)

°Riegger, Wallingford *New and Old*, #12 ("Fourths and Fifths") (also quartal)

Szymanowski, Karol *Mazurkas Op. 50, Book 1*, #2 (seconds)

Example 112
ADLER
Gradus I, #16
(m. 4-10)

Example 113
ADLER
Gradus II, #3
(m. 1-9)

Fast and furious ♩=112   [Clusters]

Excerpt from ⧧6 from *Gradus II* by SAMUEL ADLER. ¹ Copyright 1971 by Oxford University Press, Inc. Reprinted by Permission.

Vivo ♩/84   [Added Note]

Excerpt from *Fourteen Bagatelles Op. 6* by BELA BARTOK. Used by Permission of Edwin F. Kalmus.

Allegretto molto rubato   [Quartal]

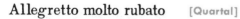

Excerpt from *Fourteen Bagatelles Op. 6* by BELA BARTOK. Used by Permission of Edwin F. Kalmus.

Example 114
ADLER
Gradus II, #6
(m. 1-6)

Example 115
BARTOK
Fourteen Bagatelles
Op. 6, #5
(m. 1-11)

Example 116
BARTOK
Fourteen Bagatelles
Op. 6, #11
(m. 1-8)

Example 117
BARTOK
Mikrokosmos, Vol. V,
#124
("Staccato")
(m. 1-7)

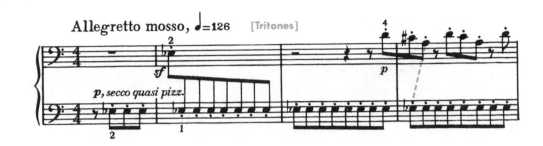

Example 118
BARTOK
Mikrokosmos, Vol. V,
#130
(m. 17-24)

Example 119
FINNEY
32 Piano Games, XI
**("3 White-Note Clusters,
High and Low")**
(m. 1-4)

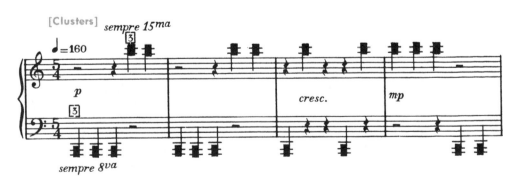

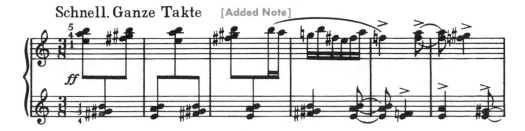

Schnell. Ganze Takte [Added Note]

Example 120
HINDEMITH
Easy Five-Tone Pieces, #5
(m. 1-6)

[Sevenths]

Example 121
STARER
Seven Vignettes, II
("Song Without Words")
(m. 32-35)

[Quintal]
tornando — al — — Tempo I° *(ma sostenuto assai)*

Example 122
BERNSTEIN
Four Anniversaries
"For David Diamond"
(m. 31-34)

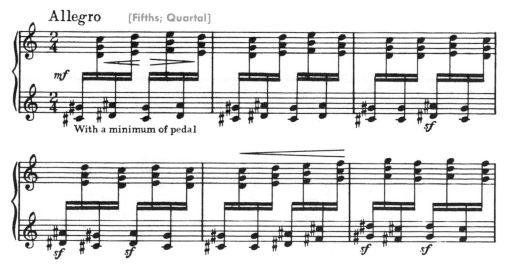

Allegro [Fifths; Quartal]

With a minimum of pedal

Example 123
RIEGGER
New and Old, #12
("Fourths and Fifths")
(m. 1-6)

Harmony 91

Melodic Doubling

Like other contemporary devices, melodic doubling has its roots in bygone centuries. It stems from ancient tenth century organum, which was the practice of "harmonizing" a melody in fourths or fifths. Undoubtedly, this style of singing grew out of the inability of some voices to reach the notes of the unison melody, that were forced to drop to a lower level. Since thirds were considered dissonant at that time, the fourth (or its inversion, the fifth) became the accepted interval. Two people can simulate this effect by singing a familiar melody in two keys a fourth apart. In Example 124, the top voice is *America* in the key of F and the lower voice is in C. (A male voice singing in F would actually sound below C, thus inverting the fourth to a fifth.)

Example 124
"America" in Organum

(The ♭ in the signature indicates only a 3rd line B♭)

Utilized by twentieth century composers as both a vocal and instrumental technic, the fourths and fifths of organum not only produce an archaic effect, but also represent a break from the recent past when parallel fifths were "not allowed," and fourths were considered unstable and, therefore, needed resolution to thirds. The stable fourth became a favorite of Hindemith who used it profusely as a melodic and harmonic constituent. Examples, such as the Tansman *Pour les Enfants* shown below, abound in piano literature for the lower grades because a small hand can easily reach these spans.

Example 125
TANSMAN
Pour les Enfants, 4th Set,
 # 4
("Cache-Cache")
(m. 1-3)

Excerpt from *Pour les Enfants, 4th Set* by ALEXANDRE TANSMAN. ' Copyright by Editions Max Eschig. Used by Permission of Associated Music Publishers.

Parallel triads are an outstanding trademark of the Russian composer Kabalevsky. In some pieces he uses them to double the melody, as in the next example.

Example 126
KABALEVSKY
Children's Pieces Op. 27
"Toccatina"
(m. 1-7)

Excerpt from *Children's Pieces Op. 27* by DMITRI KABALEVSKY. Reprinted from *Piano Literature, Vol. III.* ' Copyright 1968 by General Words and Music Company. Reprinted by Permission.

A melody doubled in thirds or sixths was very popular in the latter part of the tonal period, notably in the music of Brahms.

Example 127
BRAHMS
Waltz in A♭ Op. 39 No. 15
(m. 1-4)

The scale basis of such a passage determines whether these intervals are major or minor as they move along. Contrasting with this euphonius style are those more recent melodies which are doubled with all the same size thirds or sixths, as in this next Bartok example.

Example 128
BARTOK
Mikrokosmos, Vol. II, # 62
("Minor Sixths in Parallel
Motion")
(m. 1-6)

Excerpt from *Mikrokosmos, Vol. II* by BELA BARTOK. ' Copyright 1940 by Hawkes & Son (London) Ltd., Renewed 1967. Reprinted by Permission of Boosey & Hawkes, Inc.

The resulting chromatic "violations," known as *cross-relation,* sound delight-fully impish and spicy as though in defiance of traditional tonality that rejected them for centuries. Now, in a new environment of expanded tonality (explained in Chapter 4), there are no restrictions on cross-relation. For purposes of clarity, *America* is illustrated below with this kind of doubling.

Example 129
**Melodic Doubling of
"America"**

As sparks fly when stones are rubbed together, so a melody can be revitalized by doubling it in seconds, sevenths, tritones, or even with clusters and quartal chords. Debussy was fond of the blurring effect of seconds and often used them in conjunction with the wholetone scale. Playing *America* by ear and doubling it in these various intervals will prove to the reader how well he understands this device.

Examples of Melodic Doubling

ELEMENTARY

Adler, Samuel   *Gradus I*, #5 (fifths)

°Bartok, Bela   *Mikrokosmos, Vol. II*, #62 ("Minor Sixths in Parallel Motion") (see Example 128)

°Dello Joio, Norman   *Suite for the Young*, #8 ("A Sad Tale") (clusters)

Rollino, J., and Sheftel, P.   *Festivities*, "Ping Pong" (fourths; sevenths)

Rollino, J., and Sheftel, P.   *Festivities*, "Yoghurt" (fourths; sevenths)

Stravinsky, Soulima   *Piano Music for Children, Vol. I*, #7 ("For the kid next door") (fifths; minor sixths)

Stravinsky, Soulima   *Piano Music for Children, Vol. II*, #25 ("Pussy cat, pussy cat . . .") (triads)

INTERMEDIATE

Adler, Samuel   *Gradus II*, #3 (clusters)

°Adler, Samuel   *Gradus II*, #7 (sevenths)

Bartok, Bela   *Fourteen Bagatelles Op. 6*, #11 (quartal)

Bartok, Bela   *Mikrokosmos, Vol. III*, #73 (triads)

Bartok, Bela   *Mikrokosmos, Vol. IV*, #120 (triads)

Bartok, Bela   *Mikrokosmos, Vol. V*, #131 ("Fourths")

Bartok, Bela   *Ten Easy Pieces*, "Bear Dance" (triads)

Bartok, Bela   *Ten Easy Pieces*, "Sunrise" (major thirds)

Contemporary Collection, Revised Edition, "Etude in White" by David Kraehenbuehl (seventh chords divided between both hands)

Fennimore, Joseph   *Bits and Pieces*, "Dance of the Dinosaurs" (fourths; fifths)

Fiala, George   *Ten Postludes*, III (fourths)

Fiala, George   *Ten Postludes*, X (fifths)

°Finney, Ross Lee   *32 Piano Games*, XIX ("Berceuse") (fourths)

Fletcher, Stanley   *Street Scenes*, "Step on Every Crack" (seconds)

°Kabalevsky, Dmitri   *Children's Pieces Op. 27*, "Toccatina" (triads) (see Example 126)

°Mompou, Frederic   *Scènes d'Enfants*, "Cris dans la Rue" (quartal chords; see Example 188)

Mompou, Frederic   *Scènes d'Enfants*, "Jeune Filles au Jardin" (quartal)

Pinto, Octavio   *Scenas Infantis*, #1 ("Run, Run!") (triads; fourths)

Pinto, Octavio   *Scenas Infantis*, #4 ("Sleeping Time") (triads; added notes; fourths)

Pinto, Octavio   *Scenas Infantis*, #5 ("Hobby Horse") (fourths)

Starer, Robert   *Seven Vignettes*, I ("Fanfare") (fourths)

Stravinsky, Soulima   *Six Sonatinas*, "Sonatina Seconda," Second Movement (fifths; sevenths)

°Tansman, Alexandre   *Pour les Enfants, 4th Set*, #4 ("Cache-Cache") (fourths) (see Example 125)

ADVANCED

Bartok, Bela   *Mikrokosmos, Vol. VI*, #153 (triads)

Bartok, Bela   *Suite Op. 14*, #3 (fourths; major thirds)

Bartok, Bela   *Three Rondos*, I (triads)

Ireland, John   *Sonatina*, Second Movement (major thirds)

Kabalevsky, Dmitri   *24 Preludes Op. 38*, #2 (triads)

Kabalevsky, Dmitri   *24 Preludes Op. 38*, #4 (triads)

Kabalevsky, Dmitri   *24 Preludes Op. 38*, #24 (fifths; triads)

New Music for the Piano, "Two Preludes," #2 by Kent Kennan (fourths; fifths)

Riegger, Wallingford   *New and Old,* #2 ("The Major Second")
Riegger, Wallingford   *New and Old,* #10 ("Tone Clusters")
Riegger, Wallingford   *New and Old,* #12 ("Fourths and Fifths")
Shostakovitch, Dmitri   *L'Age d'Or,* "Polka" (ninths with added seconds)
Tcherepnin, Alexander   *Bagatelles Op. 5,* #1 (seconds)
Tcherepnin, Alexander   *Bagatelles Op. 5,* #2 (seconds)
Tcherepnin, Alexander   *Bagatelles Op. 5,* #7 (seconds)

Example 130
DELLO JOIO
Suite for the Young, # 8
("A Sad Tale")
(m. 3-8)

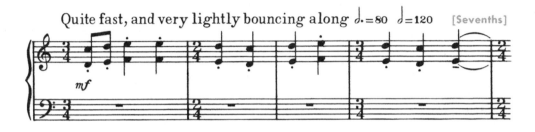

Example 131
ADLER
Gradus II, # 7
(m. 1-8)

Example 132
FINNEY
32 Piano Games, XIX
("Berceuse")
(m. 1-7)

Bichords (Polychords)

Polychords are formed when two or more chords are stacked, each one intact as a unit and spatially separated from the other. They sound simultaneously or in close association, producing a kaleidoscopic color effect and an enriched texture. Piano music abounds with *bichords*, for each hand can conveniently play a different chord. The resulting effect is most palatable to the listener because the ear is able to distinguish the individual chords, yet, at the same time, hear one grand amalgamation of sound. This sonority will vary according to the pitch-range of each chord, arrangment of tones and their root relationship (compare Example 133b with 133c and d; also 133a with 133b). In most cases, polychords or bichords are comprised of triads, sometimes seventh chords. Occasionally one finds non-tertial constructions, as in Example 133e.

Example 133
Polychords

Examples Where Bichords Are Predominant

ELEMENTARY
Persichetti, Vincent   *Parades for Piano,* "March"
Persichetti, Vincent   *Parades for Piano,* "Pomp"

INTERMEDIATE
Contemporary Piano Literature, Book 5-6, "Swinging" by Ross Lee Finney (triads based on twelve-tone row)
Finney, Ross Lee   *24 Piano Inventions,* #17 ("Dawn") (triads based on twelve-tone row)
Ginastera, Alberto   *12 American Preludes, Vol. I,* #1 ("Accents") (many non-tertial structures; some triads)
°Persichetti, Vincent   *Little Piano Book,* #10 ("Prologue") (triads)
Persichetti, Vincent   *Piano Sonatina No. 4,* Third Movement (triads; seventh chords)
°Schuman, William   *Three-Score Set,* #2 (triads)

Other Examples of Bichords

ELEMENTARY
Adler, Samuel   *Gradus I,* #15
Dello Joio, Norman   *Suite for the Young,* #2 ("Invention")
Kraehenbuehl, David   *Calendar Scenes,* #3 ("March Winds")
Olson, Lynn Freeman   *Menagerie,* "The Prickly Porcupine"
Stravinsky, Igor   *Les Cinq Doigts (The Five Fingers),* #8 (barbaric; "wrong-note" style)

INTERMEDIATE
American Composers of Today, "Night Song" by Norman Dello Joio
Bartok, Bela   *Mikrokosmos, Vol. III,* #69 ("Chord Study")
Bartok, Bela   *Mikrokosmos, Vol. III,* #73
Bartok, Bela   *Mikrokosmos, Vol. III,* #85
Bartok, Bela   *Mikrokosmos, Vol. IV,* #120
Bartok, Bela   *Mikrokosmos, Vol. V,* #122
°Bartok, Bela   *Mikrokosmos, Vol. V,* #139 ("Merry Andrew")
Contemporary Collection, Revised Edition, "Fanfares" by Gerald Shapiro (mirror writing)

Contemporary Collection, Revised Edition, "Musical Equations" by
    Frederick Koch
Contemporary Collection, Revised Edition, "Procession" by Norman
    Auerbach (mirror writing)
Dello Joio, Norman   *Lyric Pieces for the Young,* #6 ("Russian Dancer")
Goossens, Eugene   *Kaleidoscope,* "The Clockwork Dancer"
Goossens, Eugene   *Kaleidoscope,* "The Hurdy-Gurdy Man"
Goossens, Eugene   *Kaleidoscope,* "The Punch and Judy Show"

ADVANCED

Barber, Samuel   *Excursions Op. 20,* #1
Bartok, Bela   *Fourteen Bagatelles Op. 6,* #14 (seventh chords)
Bartok, Bela   *Suite Op. 14,* #4 (major thirds against each other)
Bartok, Bela   *Three Rondos,* I
Francaix, Jean   *Scherzo*
Harris, Roy   *Piano Suite*
°Harris, Roy   *Toccata* (linear and vertical; tertian and non-tertian)
Kennan, Kent   *Three Preludes,* #1 (linear and vertical)
Lloyd, Norman   *Episodes for Piano,* #3
Poulenc, Francis   *Mouvements Perpetuels,* #3 (same one repeated
    often)
Prokofiev, Serge   *Sarcasms Op. 17,* #4 (savage)
Prokofiev, Serge   *Visions Fugitives Op. 22,* #10
Shostakovitch, Dmitri   *24 Preludes Op. 34,* #12

Example 134
PERSICHETTI
***Little Piano Book,* #10**
("Prologue")
(m. 1-4)

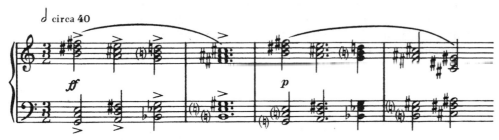

Example 135
SCHUMAN
***Three-Score Set,* #2**
(m. 1-4)

Example 136
BARTOK
Mikrokosmos, Vol. V,
#139
("Merry Andrew")
(m. 1-6)

Example 137
HARRIS
Toccata
(m. 73-74)

"Wrong-Note" Writing

No device is quite so comical as the witty *"wrong-note"* technic conceived around 1920 by Russian and French composers to voice their scorn for the chromatic and dramatic nineteenth century romanticism. Among the youthful reactionaries engaged in musical satire at this time were Prokofiev, Shostakovitch and Poulenc. They expressed their impudence in three ways: by disrupting innocent melodies with occasional "wrong" notes; in unexpected, shocking harmonizations and modulations (see Chapter 4 for "Shifted Tonality"); and in saucy, machine-like ostinatos.

Stravinsky's "wrong-note" style, on the other hand, was not so much a matter of defiance or sarcasm as it was a deliberate attempt to produce an out-of-focus effect. He accomplished this by combining incompatible intervals or chords which created strident dissonances.

Examples of "wrong-note" writing are quite common in piano music of the composers mentioned above. Others are imitations.

Examples of "Wrong-Note" Writing

ELEMENTARY
Stravinsky, Igor *Les Cinq Doigts (The Five Fingers),* #1
Stravinsky, Igor *Les Cinq Doigts (The Five Fingers),* #3
Stravinsky, Igor *Les Cinq Doigts (The Five Fingers),* #5
°Stravinsky, Igor *Les Cinq Doigts (The Five Fingers),* #8 (barbaric bichordal dissonances)

INTERMEDIATE
Goossens, Eugene *Kaleidoscope,* "The Hurdy-Gurdy Man"
Khachaturian, Aram *Adventures of Ivan,* #4 ("Ivan Goes to a Party")
Prokofiev, Serge *Children's Pieces Op. 65,* #2 ("Promenade")
Prokofiev, Serge *Children's Pieces Op. 65,* #10 ("March")
°Prokofiev, Serge *Four Pieces Op. 32,* "Gavotte"
Shostakovitch, Dmitri *Dances of the Dolls,* #1 ("Jocular Waltz")
Shostakovitch, Dmitri *Dances of the Dolls,* #7 ("Dance")
Shostakovitch, Dmitri *Three Fantastic Dances,* #2

ADVANCED
Shostakovitch, Dmitri *L'Age d'Or,* "Polka"
°Shostakovitch, Dmitri *24 Preludes Op. 34,* #6
Shostakovitch, Dmitri *24 Preludes Op. 34,* #7
Shostakovitch, Dmitri *24 Preludes Op. 34,* #8

Example 138
STRAVINSKY
Les Cinq Doigts, # 8
(m. 22-29)

Allegro non troppo

Example 139
PROKOFIEV
Four Pieces Op. 32
"Gavotte"
(m. 1-4)

Allegretto M.M. ♩=118

Example 140
SHOSTAKOVITCH
24 Preludes Op. 34, # 6
(m. 1-17)

Harmony   99

Serial Chords

A review of the section in Chapter 1 dealing with twelve-tone, serial technic is advisable as an introduction to this study.

Serial chords are derived from the sectioning of a twelve-tone row into various size groups of tones. For instance, groups of three would yield four three-note chords; groups of four would yield three four-note chords, etc.

Example 141
Twelve-Tone Row and Serial Chords

a. **Twelve-Tone Row**

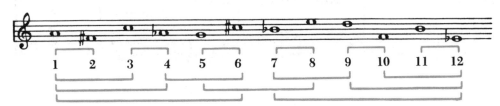

b. **Three 4-note Chords**   c. **Two 3-note Chords**   d. **Three 4-note Chords**

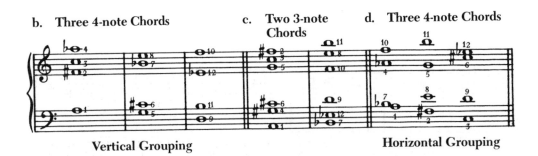

Vertical Grouping   Horizontal Grouping

A composer is free to choose more or fewer tones than twelve for his row, and also to construct his rows in a fashion that will produce the chord structures or sonorities he desires. Enharmonic spellings are common, as in Example 141c above (G♯ instead of A♭). Derivations of the row—inversion, retrograde, transposition, retrograde inversion—may also be sectioned for building chords. The tones may be placed in any order vertically and are usually spaced in an open manner to avoid clusters which would destroy the contrapuntal texture so idiomatic to the bulk of serial writing. Exceptions will be found.

Examples of Serial Chords

INTERMEDIATE

Contemporary Piano Literature, Book 5-6, "Swinging" by Ross Lee Finney (groups of three arranged in polychords; original and retrograde versions of row)

°Finney, Ross Lee   *24 Piano Inventions,* #17 ("Dawn") (groups of three arranged in polychords; original and retrograde versions of row)

Finney, Ross Lee   *24 Piano Inventions,* #18 ("Walking") (groups of two in retrograde)

°Krenek, Ernst   *12 Short Piano Pieces Op. 83,* #4 ("The Moon Rises")

ADVANCED

New Music for the Piano, "Six Preludes," #4 by George Perle (groups of five, five and two)

Schoenberg, Arnold   *Klavierstuck Op. 33a*

°Schoenberg, Arnold   *Suite für Klavier Op. 25,* "Gavotte"

Webern, Anton   *Variations Op. 27, I*

Webern, Anton   *Variations Op. 27, III*

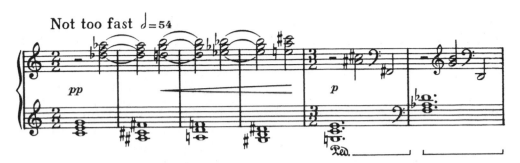

Excerpt from *24 Piano Inventions* by ROSS LEE FINNEY (P 66262). ' Copyright 1971 by Henmar Press, Inc., 373 Park Avenue South, New York, New York 10016.
Reprint permission granted by the publisher.

Example 142
FINNEY
24 Piano Inventions, # 17
("Dawn")
(m. 1-6)

Excerpt from *12 Short Piano Pieces Op. 83* by ERNST KRENEK. Copyright by G. Schirmer, Inc. Used by Permission.

Example 143
KRENEK
12 Short Piano Pieces
Op. 83, # 4
("The Moon Rises")
(m. 1-4)

Excerpt from *Suite für Klavier Op. 25* by ARNOLD SCHOENBERG. ' Copyright 1925 by Universal Edition. Copyright renewed 1952 by Gertrude Schoenberg.
Used by Permission of Belmont Music Publishers, Los Angeles, California 90049.

Example 144
SCHOENBERG
Suite für Klavier Op. 25
"Gavotte"
(m. 22-23)

Harmonics

Peculiar to piano music is the recent device of depressing some keys silently while playing others. A word of explanation usually accompanies the "silent" diamond or triangular-shaped notes which indicate this device. Bartok's terminology, "harmonics," originates from the *harmonic series of overtones* which is the acoustical basis for the resulting sound. The following example illustrates the overtones generated by the tone "C."

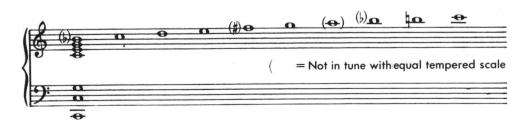

(= Not in tune with equal tempered scale

Example 145
Harmonic Series of
Overtones

The resonance and quality of a tone are determined by the number of overtones which are audible. This accounts for the fact that tones in the upper register of the piano sound thinner and are of shorter duration than those in the lower register.

When keys are depressed silently, the raised dampers allow the strings to sympathetically vibrate when other notes are played. The result is a mixture of sound. It is conjecture on the writer's part that Beethoven may have been one of the first to explore this device—toward the end of the first movement of his *Piano Sonata Op. 31 No. 2.* Here, the left hand chord is played and then held down (with or without pedal), but the effect is similar to that of harmonics .

Example 146
BEETHOVEN
Sonata Op. 31 No. 2
First Movement
(m. 143-148)

A few examples of *harmonics* in modern piano music are cited below. Perhaps the reader can find more.

Examples of Harmonics

ELEMENTARY
   Adventures in Time and Space, Vol. I, "I Hear an Echo" by Mary Mageau
   °Kraehenbuehl, David   *Calendar Scenes,* #5 ("Memorial")

INTERMEDIATE
   °Bartok, Bela   *Mikrokosmos, Vol. IV,* #102 ("Harmonics")
   Horizons, Book 1, "Elegy for a Misty Afternoon" by Brian Cherney
   °Krenek, Ernst   *12 Short Piano Pieces Op. 83,* #10 ("On the High Mountains")
   Pentland, Barbara   *Echoes,* I
   Pentland, Barbara   *Echoes,* II

ADVANCED
   Britten, Benjamin   *Night-Music* (final chord)
   Cowell, Henry   *Piano Music,* "Tiger"

Example 147
KRAEHENBUEHL
***Calendar Scenes,* #5**
("Memorial")
(m. 1-6)

⁵⁄₃ L. H. press down silently and hold.

Excerpt from *Calendar Scenes* by DAVID KRAEHENBUEHL. Used by permission of the publishers, Schmitt, Hall & McCreary Company.

Allegro non troppo, un poco rubato, ♩=ca 110

Example 148
BARTOK
Mikrokosmos, Vol. IV,
102
("Harmonics")
(m. 1-15)

to be depressed silently

Example 149
KRENEK
12 Short Piano Pieces
Op. 83, # 10
("On the High
Mountains")
(m. 10-13)

In the roster of orchestral instruments the piano assumes its place in the percussion section due to the way the tone is produced—hammers *strike* the strings. From the scintillating runs of Mozart to the romantic lyricism of Chopin, from the passionate harmonies of Beethoven to the delicate atmosphere of Debussy, one finds little evidence of the piano living up to its family name. On the contrary, the conscientious pianist labors arduously to develop a fortissimo that is not "banging."

**Percussive Use
of Harmony**

But in the twentieth century, composers are deliberately exploiting the percussive properties of the piano, as they have of the string, woodwind and brass instruments. (This is most evident in the orchestral music of Stravinsky and Bartok.) For the last piece of his *Suite for Piano "1922" Op. 26*, entitled "Ragtime," Hindemith gives the following instructions, "Don't pay any attention to what you learned in your piano lessons! . . . Play this piece very savagely, but always rigidly in rhythm like a machine. Consider the piano as an interesting kind of percussion instrument and treat it accordingly."[8]

Common means for creating this dynamic, sometimes brutal effect are tone clusters, use of the low register, and large splashes of skyscraper-like chords (the latter, mainly orchestral). Combinations of these or a driving rhythmic texture intensifies the degree of percussion. Dynamics also play a significant role, though not all percussive effects are necessarily loud.

Examples of Percussive Use of Harmony

INTERMEDIATE

°Bartok, Bela   *Mikrokosmos, Vol. IV,* #116 ("Melody")
Bartok, Bela   *Mikrokosmos, Vol. V,* #122
°Pinto, Octavio   *Scenas Infantis,* #3 ("March, Little Soldier")

ADVANCED

Bartok, Bela   *Allegro Barbaro* (chordal with seconds; loud)
Bartok, Bela   *Mikrokosmos, Vol. VI,* #142
°Bartok, Bela   *Mikrokosmos, Vol. VI,* #146 ("Ostinato")
Bartok, Bela   *Mikrokosmos, Vol. VI,* #147
Bartok, Bela   *Mikrokosmos, Vol. VI,* #149
°Bartok, Bela   *Three Rondos,* III
Bernstein, Leonard   *Four Anniversaries,* "For Helen Coates"
Cowell, Henry   *Piano Music,* "Exultation"
Cowell, Henry   *Piano Music,* "The Tides of Manaunaun"
Cowell, Henry   *Piano Music,* "Tiger"
Hindemith, Paul   *Suite for Piano "1922" Op. 26,* "Ragtime"
Prokofiev, Serge   *Sarcasms Op. 17*
°Prokofiev, Serge   *Visions Fugitives Op. 22,* #14

DIFFICULT

Prokofiev, Serge   *Suggestion Diabolique*

Example 150
BARTOK
Mikrokosmos, Vol. IV,
#116
("Melody")
(m. 1-8)

Excerpt from Mikrokosmos, Vol. IV by BELA BARTOK ° Copyright 1940 by Hawkes & Son (London) Ltd., Renewed 1967. Reprinted by Permission of Boosey & Hawkes, Inc.

---

[8]Peter Hansen, *An Introduction to Twentieth Century Music,* p. 264.

Example 151
PINTO
Scenas Infantis, #3
("March, Little Soldier")
(m. 20-24)

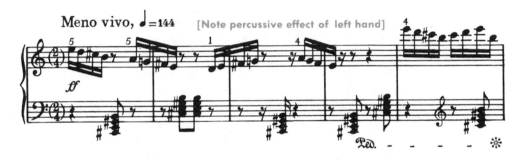

Meno vivo, ♩=144   [Note percussive effect of left hand]

Example 152
BARTOK
Mikrokosmos, Vol. VI, #146
("Ostinato")
(m. 81-85)

Allegro molto, ♩=144   poco rit. _ _ _

Example 153
BARTOK
Three Rondos, III
(m. 1-5)

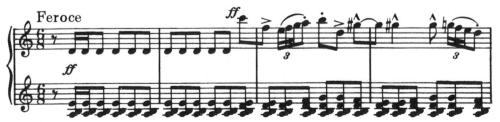

Feroce

Example 154
PROKOFIEV
Visions Fugitives Op. 22,
#14
(m. 1-4)

Suggested Assignments

1. Play and study a representative sampling of the piano pieces listed.

2. For additional resource reading, consult the following:

   Dallin *Techniques of Twentieth Century Composition,* Chapters 6, 7 and 11.
   Persichetti *Twentieth-Century Harmony*
   Ulehla *Contemporary Harmony*

3. Listen to the following complete works, with score if possible:

   Bartok *Concerto for Orchestra* (melodic doubling)
   Bartok *String Quartet No. 2,* First and Second Movements (cross-relations; tritones; sevenths)
   Bartok *String Quartet No. 4,* First Movement (percussive blocks of sound, m. 58-92)
   Honegger *King David* (Play the score, especially pages 1, 9, 15, 25, 70-75, 85, 93, for quartal, quintal and tertian complex chords, fourths, ostinato, polychords, parallel triads.)
   Honegger *Symphony No. 5,* First Movement (polychords)
   Ives *Piano Sonata No. 2* (polychords)
   Ives *Sonata No. 2 for Violin and Piano,* Third Movement (complex chords)
   Persichetti *Divertimento for Band,* Sixth Movement (polychords)
   Shostakovitch *L'Age d'Or,* "Polka" ("wrong" notes)
   Shostakovitch *Symphony No. 5,* Second Movement ("wrong" notes)
   Stravinsky *L'Histoire du Soldat,* "Great Chorale" (Analyze the score. Look for narrow melodies, linear counterpoint, "wrong" notes, modal effects, seventh and ninth chords, voices moving in sevenths [m. 17-18], treatment of non-chordals.)
   Stravinsky *Petrouchka,* "Dance of the Nuns" (parallelism)
   Stravinsky *Petrouchka,* "Russian Dance" (parallelism)

4. Experiment at the piano with different sonorities of polychords, harmonics and sound effects resulting from the depressed damper pedal picking up sympathetic vibrations of various inside and outside-of-the-piano noises or pitches.

5. Write several short studies, each one based upon one or more harmonic devices.

Chapter 4
Tonality and Modality

As previously mentioned, the tonal system during the seventeenth, eighteenth and nineteenth centuries was based upon the familiar seven-tone major and minor scales with the first note, the tonic, functioning as the strong point of gravitation and final rest. All chords bear a particular relationship with the tonic and are connected into meaningful groups, much the same as words, functioning as nouns, verbs, adjectives and adverbs are selected and arranged into phrases, sentences and paragraphs to convey ideas.

In the classic period, chromatic chords were employed decoratively, with the diatonic chords, principally tonic, subdominant and dominant, providing the basic framework by which the tonality was established. During the nineteenth century, or romantic era, chromatic harmony became much more prevalent until it constituted the very warp and woof of musical expression. It was Wagner's skillful manipulation of extreme chromaticism and of evaded or deceptive cadences to create dramatic effects of suspense, tension and heightened emotion in his late operas—*Tristan und Isolde* and *Parsifal*—that weakened tonality to the point of its eventual breakdown. Other works of consequence could be cited, such as the opera, *Boris Godunov* by Mussorgsky, which is reputed to have had a profound influence on the young Debussy.

By the turn-of-the-century, primary triads—the pillars of tonality—were being de-emphasized, and non-functional harmony was replacing the traditional, further undermining the old tonal system. Subsequently, three significant compositional trends developed signalling the collapse of tonality. Respectively, these repudiated, adopted and organized chromaticism. *Modality* and *pan-diatonicism* characterized the first trend; *expanded* and *shifted tonality*, and *free atonality*, the second; and *polytonality* and *serial atonality*, the last. It becomes evident, then, that the degrees of tonality in today's music extend all the way from the presence of a tonal center, to more than one key at a time, to no tonality at all.

Before studying these various technics separately, a word should be said about *key signatures*. In much contemporary music they have outgrown their usefulness, for they are the sign of tonal (or modal) music. With the disintegration of tonality comes also the discarding of traditional key signatures. Their absence is usually due to the fact that modulations occur too frequently, that expanded tonality utilizes all twelve tones, or that atonality prevails. It is easier to eliminate a key signature and assume an accidental refers *only* to that particular note, than to be constantly adding accidentals for both altering and cancelling purposes.

Where synthetic scales form the primary basis of the music, *new* key signatures have been devised. Bartok is noted for including only those accidentals which will be encountered in the piece and positioning them on the precise line or space they occur. Other composers have also exercised their independence in the formulation of novel key signatures. Thus, traditional signatures may be incomplete or partially disguised by a new arrangement.

Works with no key signature are too numerous to be mentioned, but some that contain new signatures are included here for reference.

Examples of New Key Signatures

ELEMENTARY
°Bartok, Bela   *Mikrokosmos, Vol. I,* #10 (synthetic)
°Bartok, Bela   *Mikrokosmos, Vol. I,* #25 (synthetic)
Bartok, Bela   *Mikrokosmos, Vol. II,* #38 (new arrangement)
°Bartok, Bela   *Mikrokosmos, Vol. II,* #40 (new arrangement)
Bartok, Bela   *Mikrokosmos, Vol. II,* #41 (synthetic)
Bartok, Bela   *Mikrokosmos, Vol. II,* #50 (incomplete)

INTERMEDIATE
Bartok, Bela   *For Children, Vol. II,* #32 (synthetic)
Bartok, Bela   *Mikrokosmos, Vol. III,* #89 (incomplete; new arrangement)
Bartok, Bela   *Mikrokosmos, Vol. IV,* #99 (bitonal; incomplete; new arrangement)
°Mompou, Frederic   *Scènes d'Enfants,* "Cris dans la Rue" (new; given only once for four scores)
°Starer, Robert   *Seven Vignettes,* VI ("The Camel and the Moon") (synthetic)
°Toch, Ernst   *Three Little Dances Op. 85,* #1 (new arrangement)

Example 155
BARTOK
Mikrokosmos, Vol. I, #10
(m. 1-7)

Example 156
BARTOK
Mikrokosmos, Vol. I, #25
(m. 1-9)

Example 157
BARTOK
Mikrokosmos, Vol. II, #40
(m. 1-6)

Example 158
MOMPOU
Scènes d'Enfants
"Cris dans la Rue"
(m. 13-17)

Example 159
STARER
Seven Vignettes, VI
("The Camel and the Moon")
(m. 1-3)

Example 160
TOCH
Three Little Dances
Op. 85, #1
(m. 1-2)

Tonality and Modality   109

Modality

As stated in Chapter 1, modality formed the basis of music from Grecian times in sixth century B.C. up to the ascendancy of the major-minor tonal system in 1600. Except for Bach's harmonizations of modal chorale melodies, the modes succumbed to dormancy that lasted well into the nineteenth century, when Chopin employed them in some of his *Mazurkas*. Later, Brahms showed a predilection for an occasional use of modalism as did Mussorgsky, Dvorak, Sibelius, Franck and Grieg. So it was no surprise that Debussy, in the vanguard of modern music, should add the modes to his palette of new melodic resource along with wholetone, pentatonic and other exotic scales.

Since the turn-of-the-century, modalism has continued to thrive. Its comparative simplicity and unpretentious character make it readily accessible to all and, therefore, it continues to be idiomatic in folk song style. The *Oxford Book of Carols*, a compilation of British sacred and secular folk songs, provides a wealth of contemporary modal settings which the reader is urged to play.

Contemporary modalism differs fundamentally from previous modal textures. For, during the Greek and Early Christian eras, modalism was *monodic*—a single melodic line; in the Medieval and Renaissance periods it was *polyphonic*—more than one melody sounding simultaneously; but in this century it is *harmonic*—modal melodies harmonized with progressions from the major-minor system, including many seventh and ninth chords. The resultant vertical and dissonant texture is called "neo-modalism" or the new modalism.

However, all contemporary modalism is not dissonant. For the nineteenth century concept, which has been carried over into the twentieth, seems to have consisted chiefly of melodic inflections or modal cadences within a predominantly tonal framework, as the following examples illustrate.

Example 161
CHOPIN
Mazurka # 15 Op. 24
No. 2
(m. 25-28)

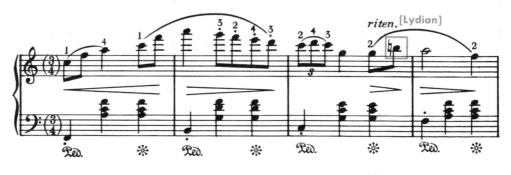

Example 162
CHOPIN
Mazurka # 26 Op. 41
No. 1
(m. 1-4)

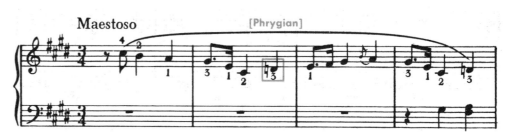

Example 163
BRAHMS
Rhapsody Op. 119 No. 4
(m. 257-262)

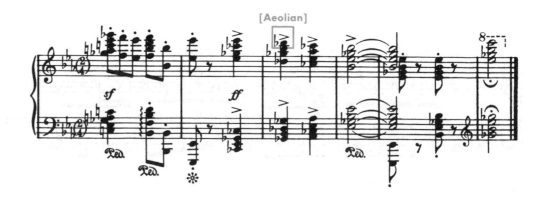

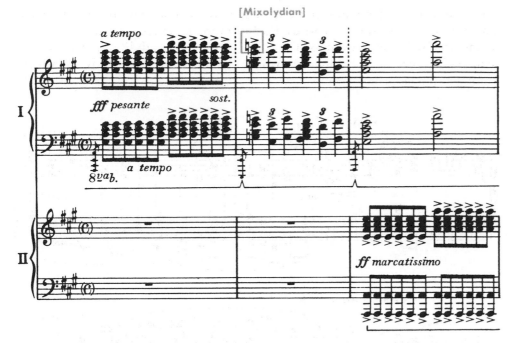

Example 164
GRIEG
Piano Concerto in A Minor
Op. 16
Third Movement
(m. 8-6 from the end)

Excerpt from *Piano Concerto in A Minor Op. 16* by EDVARD GRIEG. Copyright by G. Schirmer, Inc. Used by Permission.

As a general rule, cadential progressions consist of chords containing the note(s) that distinguishes the mode from a major or minor scale. For instance, IV-i and ii-i mark the Dorian mode; vii-i, v°-i and II-i, Phrygian; II-I, Lydian; VII-I and v-I, Mixolydian; v-i, Aeolian; ending on i°, Locrian; V-I, Ionian. (Key to analysis symbols: I = major; i = minor; i° = diminished.)

Example 165
Modal Progressions

One also observes that many modal melodies are associated with non-functional harmony or non-tertian structures. Furthermore, a "pseudo-modalism" which is effected by an emphasis upon the minor secondary triads (ii, iii, vi) or regression (V-IV) may be found in some works. Such texture is apt to be relatively simple and consonant.

Example 166
DEBUSSY
Preludes, Book 1, # 8
("La fille aux cheveux de lin")
(m. 23-31)

Excerpt from *Preludes, Book 1* by CLAUDE DEBUSSY. ᶜ Copyright 1910 by Durand et Cie. Used by permission of the publisher. Elkan-Vogel, Inc, sole representative, United States.

Example 167
RAVEL
Pavane pour une infante défunte
(m. 1-6)

Excerpt from *Pavane pour une infante défunte* by Maurice Ravel. Reprinted from *51 Piano Pieces from the Modern Repertoire*. Copyright by G. Schirmer, Inc. Used by Permission.

Pianists are especially indebted to Kabalevsky and Bartok for producing such a quantity of modal music for the early grades. Some are harmonic in texture and some polyphonic. Among the pieces listed below, Bartok's *Mikrokosmos, Vols. I* and *II*, Mary Elizabeth Clark's *Contempo* books and *In the Mode*, and Steven's *Six Modal Miniatures* have pertinent pedagogical value. Turn back to Chapter 1 for a more comprehensive and itemized listing of modal music.

Turn back to Chapter 1 for a more comprehensive and itemized listing of modal music.

Examples of Modality

ELEMENTARY

Adler, Samuel   *Gradus I,* #4
°Adler, Samuel   *Gradus I,* #7
Adler, Samuel   *Gradus I,* #14
Bartok, Bela   *Mikrokosmos, Vol. I*
Bartok, Bela   *Mikrokosmos, Vol. II*
°*Contempo 1,* "The Child" (Mixolydian)
°*Contempo 1,* "Sad Mood" by Billie Ferrell (Phrygian)
°*Contempo 1,* "The Workshop" by D. Jaeger Bres (Lydian)
°*Contempo 2,* "Those Silly Clocks" by Anne Shannon Demarest (Locrian)
Contempos in Crimson, ed. by Mary Elizabeth Clark
Contempos in Jade, ed. by Mary Elizabeth Clark
Kabalevsky, Dmitri   *24 Little Pieces for Children Op. 39,* #3
Kabalevsky, Dmitri   *24 Little Pieces for Children Op. 39,* #4
°Kabalevsky, Dmitri   *24 Little Pieces for Children Op. 39,* #8
Kabalevsky, Dmitri   *24 Little Pieces for Children Op. 39,* #9
Kabalevsky, Dmitri   *24 Little Pieces for Children Op. 39,* #22
Stevens, Everett   *Six Modal Miniatures*
Stravinsky, Soulima   *Piano Music for Children, Vol. I,* #12 ("Pastoral tune")
Stravinsky, Soulima   *Piano Music for Children, Vol. I,* #13 ("Wistful")
Stravinsky, Soulima   *Piano Music for Children, Vol. I,* #16 ("Tricycle")
°Stravinsky, Soulima   *Piano Music for Children, Vol. I,* #18 ("On the way to school")
Stravinsky, Soulima   *Piano Music for Children, Vol. II,* #20 ("First date")
Stravinsky, Soulima   *Piano Music for Children, Vol. II,* #28 ("Answering back")

INTERMEDIATE

Bartok, Bela   *Roumanian Folk Dances*
Bloch, Ernest   *Enfantines*
Casella, Alfredo   *11 Children's Pieces*
In the Mode, ed. by Mary Elizabeth Clark
Kabalevsky, Dmitri   *Children's Pieces Op. 27*
Kabalevsky, Dmitri   *Sonatina Op. 13 No. 1*

Example 168
ADLER
Gradus I, #7
(m. 1-4)

Excerpt from #7 from *Gradus I* by SAMUEL ADLER. Copyright 1971 by Oxford University Press, Inc. Reprinted by Permission.

Example 169
FOLK SONG
The Child
(m. 11-16)

[Mixolydian]

Example 170
FERRELL
Sad Mood
(m. 14-22)

[Phrygian]

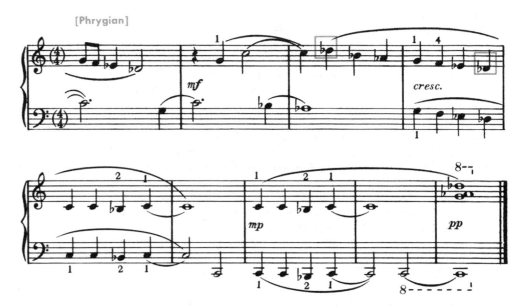

Example 171
BRES
The Workshop
(m. 42-47)

[Lydian]

Example 172
DEMAREST
Those Silly Clocks
(m. 16-19)

[Locrian]

Example 173
KABALEVSKY
24 Little Pieces for
Children Op. 39, #8
(m. 5-8)

Example 174
STRAVINSKY, S.
Piano Music for Children,
Vol. I, #18
("On the way to school")
(m. 4-8)

Bitonality and Bimodality

Reaction against chromaticism resulted in a type of organization whereby two keys or two modes sound simultaneously in separate layers; in the case of piano music, one in each hand. The use of two keys is called *bitonality* and the use of two modes, *bimodality*. The latter means either two different modes, as Lydian and Aeolian, or major and minor, as G major and g minor. As with the major-minor chord, the minor is usually on top. The term, *polytonality*, is used interchangeably with bitonality, but in a stricter sense refers to more than two tonal streams, which practically limits it to orchestral textures. Melodic doubling at the same interval is automatically bitonal, though not always obvious to the ear (i.e., Examples 124 and 129 in Chapter 3).

The general effect of these combined tonalities is a novel one, often humorous or satirical, and therefore, is usually short-lived. Key signatures may or may not be the same for each staff.

Variations of this device are formed when one hand plays *white* notes and the other *black;* or when two *synthetic* scales generate different "tonalities."

Polytonality became an important feature in the musical style of Darius Milhaud, while other composers before and after him used it to a lesser degree. His most exemplary piano work is the two-volume *Saudades do Brazil* for the advanced pianist. For the young student, however, there is a fine collection called *Ten Polytonal Compositions* by William Fichandler. This is particularly useful because of the instructive material which accompanies each piece.

Examples of Bitonality and Bimodality

ELEMENTARY
    Adler, Samuel   *Gradus I,* #10
    Adler, Samuel   *Gradus I,* #12
Adventures in Time and Space, Vol. I, "Fife and Drum" by Mary
        Mageau (black and white)
    Bartok, Bela   *Mikrokosmos, Vol. II,* #59
    Bartok, Bela   *Mikrokosmos, Vol. II,* #66
°Dello Joio, Norman   *Suite for the Young,* #6 ("Echoes")

Rollino, J., and Sheftel, P. *Festivities*, "Hold Your Own"
°Stravinsky, Igor *Les Cinq Doigts (The Five Fingers)*, #6
°Stravinsky, Soulima *Piano Music for Children, Vol. I*, #8 ("Tag")

INTERMEDIATE

Adler, Samuel *Gradus II*, #6 (black and white)
American Composers of Today, "Parade" by Joseph Prostakoff
American Composers of Today, "Walk" by Miriam Gideon
Bartok, Bela *Fourteen Bagatelles Op. 6*, #1
Bartok, Bela *Fourteen Bagatelles Op. 6*, #7 (or advanced level)
Bartok, Bela *Fourteen Bagatelles Op. 6*, #10 (or advanced level)
Bartok, Bela *Mikrokosmos, Vol. III*, #70
Bartok, Bela *Mikrokosmos, Vol. III*, #71
Bartok, Bela *Mikrokosmos, Vol. III*, #79
Bartok, Bela *Mikrokosmos, Vol. III*, #81
Bartok, Bela *Mikrokosmos, Vol. III*, #86
Bartok, Bela *Mikrokosmos, Vol. III*, #90
Bartok, Bela *Mikrokosmos, Vol. IV*, #99
Bartok, Bela *Mikrokosmos, Vol. IV*, #101
Bartok, Bela *Mikrokosmos, Vol. IV*, #103
Bartok, Bela *Mikrokosmos, Vol. IV*, #104
Bartok, Bela *Mikrokosmos, Vol. IV*, #105
Bartok, Bela *Mikrokosmos, Vol. IV*, #110
Bartok, Bela *Mikrokosmos, Vol. IV*, #117
Bartok, Bela *Mikrokosmos, Vol. IV*, #121
Bartok, Bela *Mikrokosmos, Vol. V*, #125 ("Boating")
°Bartok, Bela *Mikrokosmos, Vol. V*, #131 ("Fourths")
Bartok, Bela *Mikrokosmos, Vol. V*, #136
Casella, Alfredo *11 Children's Pieces*, I ("Preludio")
°Casella, Alfredo *11 Children's Pieces*, IX ("Carillon") (black and white)
Contemporary Collection, Revised Edition, "Evening Song" by Gerald Shapiro
Contemporary Collection, Revised Edition, "Siciliana" by Robert Keys Clark
Contemporary Collection, Revised Edition, "Three Short Pieces," III by Hugh Aitken
°Creston, Paul *Five Little Dances*, "Pastoral Dance"
°Fichandler, William *Ten Polytonal Compositions*, "Day Dreams"
°Fichandler, William *Ten Polytonal Compositions*, "A Melody"
Fletcher, Stanley *Street Scenes*, "My Shadow Does What I Do"
Fletcher, Stanley *Street Scenes*, "Night Patrol"
Fletcher, Stanley *Street Scenes*, "Sparrows"
Masters of Our Day, "A Day-Dream" by Virgil Thomson
Persichetti, Vincent *Little Piano Book*, #7 ("Humoreske")
Pinto, Octavio *Scenas Infantis*, #4 ("Sleeping Time")
Pinto, Octavio *Scenas Infantis*, #5 ("Hobby Horse")
Rea, John *What You Will* (polytonal duets)
Starer, Robert *Sketches in Color*, #1 ("Purple")
Starer, Robert *Sketches in Color*, #3 ("Black and White")
Studies in 20th Century Idioms, "Black and White" by E. Rathburn

ADVANCED

Bartok, Bela *Allegro Barbaro* (some)
°Milhaud, Darius *Saudades do Brazil, Book 2*, #7 ("Corcovado")
°Milhaud, Darius *Saudades do Brazil, Book 2*, #8 ("Tijuca")
Prokofiev, Serge *Sarcasms Op. 17*, #3
Poulenc, Francis *Mouvements Perpetuels*, #1
Riegger, Wallingford *New and Old*, #11 ("Polytonality")

DIFFICULT

Barber, Samuel *Nocturne* (some)

Example 175
DELLO JOIO
Suite for the Young, # 6
("Echoes")
(m. 5-7)

Example 176
STRAVINSKY
Les Cinq Doigts, # 6
(m. 1-4)

Example 177
STRAVINSKY, S.
Piano Music for Children,
Vol. I, # 8
("Tag")
(m. 1-8)

Example 178
BARTOK
Mikrokosmos, Vol. V, # 131
("Fourths")
(m. 1-10)

Example 179
CASELLA
11 Children's Pieces, IX
("Carillon")
(m. 1-6)

Example 180
CRESTON
Five Little Dances
"Pastoral Dance"
(m. 1-8)

Example 181
FICHANDLER
Ten Polytonal Compositions
"Day Dreams"
(m. 1-4)

Example 182
FICHANDLER
*Ten Polytonal
Compositions
"A Melody"*
(m. 1-6)

Excerpt from *Ten Polytonal Compositions* by WILLIAM FICHANDLER. Reprinted by permission of Belwin-Mills Publishing Corporation, Melville, New York, the copyright owner.

Example 183
MILHAUD
*Saudades do Brazil,
Book 2, #7
("Corcovado")*
(m. 1-9)

Excerpt from *Saudades do Brazil, Book 2* by DARIUS MILHAUD. Permission for use authorized by Belwin-Mills Publishing Corporation, exclusive U.S. agents for Schott and Company.

Example 184
MILHAUD
*Saudades do Brazil,
Book 2, #8
("Tijuca")*
(m. 39-42)

Excerpt from *Saudades do Brazil, Book 2* by DARIUS MILHAUD. Permission for use authorized by Belwin-Mills Publishing Corporation, exclusive U.S. agents for Schott and Company.

Pandiatonicism

Pandiatonicism also came about as a reaction against chromaticism. It is often referred to as "white-note" writing because all or most of the tones are derived from one scale, frequently major. In fact, some composers, like Prokofiev, deliberately chose the key of C at a time when the bulk of music was black with accidentals.[9] Though traditional chord progressions are avoided, endings are on the tonic. The texture is usually contrapuntal and chords are tertian or non-tertian in structure. An ostinato may even be present. Because of the limited sound possibilities, a pandiatonic passage is often of short duration.

Some of the examples given below are not strictly pandiatonic (some contain harmonic texture or traditional cadences, etc.), but are similar enough to justify their inclusion here.

Examples of Pandiatonicism

ELEMENTARY

Kabalevsky, Dmitri   *24 Little Pieces for Children Op. 39,* #12
Kabalevsky, Dmitri   *24 Little Pieces for Children Op. 39,* #15
Kabalevsky, Dmitri   *24 Little Pieces for Children Op. 39,* #18
Stravinsky, Igor   *Les Cinq Doigts (The Five Fingers),* #1
Stravinsky, Igor   *Les Cinq Doigts (The Five Fingers),* #2
°Stravinsky, Igor   *Les Cinq Doigts (The Five Fingers),* #3

INTERMEDIATE

Contemporary Collection, Revised Edition, "Etude in White" by David Kraehenbuehl
°Dello Joio, Norman   *Lyric Pieces for the Young,* #3 ("Street Cries")
°Lloyd, Norman   *Episodes for Piano,* #5
°Mompou, Frederic   *Scènes d'Enfants,* "Cris dans la Rue"
Pinto, Octavio   *Scenas Infantis,* #1 ("Run, Run!")
°Toch, Ernst   *Three Little Dances Op. 85,* #2

ADVANCED

Chavez, Carlos   *Ten Preludes* (modal contexts)
Poulenc, Francis   *Trois Pieces,* "Toccata"

Example 185
STRAVINSKY
***Les Cinq Doigts,* #3**
(m. 1-16)

Excerpt from *Les Cinq Doigts* by IGOR STRAVINSKY. Reprinted with kind permission of J & W Chester/Edition Wilhelm Hansen London Limited.

[9]Peter Hansen, *An Introduction to Twentieth Century Music,* p. 288.

Gaily ♩=69

Example 186
DELLO JOIO
Lyric Pieces for the Young,
#3 ("Street Cries")
(m. 1-5)

Gaily (♩=c. 132–144)

Example 187
LLOYD
Episodes for Piano, #5
(m. 1-8)

Tonality and Modality **121**

Example 188
MOMPOU
Scènes d'Enfants
"Cris dans la Rue"
(m. 1-9)

Excerpt from *Scènes d'Enfants* by FREDERIC MOMPOU. ° Copyright 1921, Maurice Senart. Used by Permission of the publisher, Editions Salabert.

Example 189
TOCH
Three Little Dances
Op. 85, #2
(m. 1-8)

Excerpt from *Three Little Dances Op. 85* by ERNST TOCH. Used by permission of Belwin-Mills Publishing Corporation, Melville, New York.

Shifted tonality simply means a sudden modulation to a distant key, as D to E♭, and represents a repudiation of the lengthy modulatory passages in nineteenth century music. It is an idiosyncrasy of Soviet composers, notably Shostakovitch and Prokofiev, who employ it in a capricious manner much the same way they use "wrong-note" harmony.

As the name implies, *shifted tonality* occurs in a strong tonal context, and the harmony which accompanies it is uncomplicated. The new key is of short duration and seldom is well-established before darting back to the original tonality or on to a new one.

ELEMENTARY
    Dello Joio, Norman   *Suite for the Young,* #5 ("Lullaby")
    Dello Joio, Norman   *Suite for the Young,* #7 ("Bagatelle")
  °Shostakovitch, Dmitri   *Six Children's Pieces,* #6 ("The Mechanical Doll") (all the pieces contain shifted tonality)

INTERMEDIATE
    Fiala, George   *Ten Postludes,* VI
  °Prokofiev, Serge   *Children's Pieces Op. 65,* #2 ("Promenade")
    Prokofiev, Serge   *Children's Pieces Op. 65,* #11 ("Evening")
    Prokofiev, Serge   *Four Pieces Op. 32,* "Gavotte"
  °Shostakovitch, Dmitri   *Dances of the Dolls,* #2 ("Gavotte")
    Shostakovitch, Dmitri   *Dances of the Dolls,* #3 ("Romance")
    Shostakovitch, Dmitri   *Three Fantastic Dances,* #3
    Toch, Ernst   *Reflections Op. 86,* #5

ADVANCED
  °Prokofiev, Serge   *Visions Fugitives Op. 22,* #5
    Shostakovitch, Dmitri   *24 Preludes Op. 34,* #5
  °Shostakovitch, Dmitri   *24 Preludes Op. 34,* #6
    Shostakovitch, Dmitri   *24 Preludes Op. 34,* #10
    Shostakovitch, Dmitri   *24 Preludes Op. 34,* #12
    Shostakovitch, Dmitri   *24 Preludes Op. 34,* #15
    Shostakovitch, Dmitri   *24 Preludes Op. 34,* #16
    Shostakovitch, Dmitri   *24 Preludes Op. 34,* #18
    Shostakovitch, Dmitri   *24 Preludes Op. 34,* #19
    Shostakovitch, Dmitri   *24 Preludes Op. 34,* #20
    Shostakovitch, Dmitri   *24 Preludes Op. 34,* #21

Example 190
SHOSTAKOVITCH
Six Children's Pieces, #6
("The Mechanical Doll")
(m. 20-27)

Excerpt from *Six Children's Pieces* by DMITRI SHOSTAKOVITCH. Used by Permission of Edwin F. Kalmus.

[*] = **Start of new key**

Example 191
PROKOFIEV
Children's Pieces Op. 65,
#2 ("Promenade")
(m. 13-25)

Example 192
SHOSTAKOVITCH
Dances of the Dolls, #2
("Gavotte")
(m. 16-25)

Example 193
PROKOFIEV
Visions Fugitives Op. 22,
#5
(m. 1-6a)

124   *Tonality and Modality*

Example 194
SHOSTAKOVITCH
24 Preludes Op. 34, #6
(m. 18-28)

Excerpt from *24 Preludes Op. 34* by DMITRI SHOSTAKOVITCH. Copyright by G. Schirmer, Inc. Used by Permission.

Expanded Tonality

Settling on a term for this tonal system is problematic and of doubtful consequence. One finds *free tonality, expanded tonality* and *extended tonality* all used to describe the kind of tonality which is based upon the dodecuple scale but which has a *key center* and ends on a "tonic." (*Free atonality* has *no* key center, though the line of distinction is sometimes very fine.) All twelve tones are used freely throughout the work so the tonality is often not predictable until the cadence, or even the last chord. Hindemith and Bartok are the outstanding composers utilizing this technic.

Examples of Expanded Tonality

INTERMEDIATE

Adler, Samuel   *Gradus II, #4*
Adler, Samuel   *Gradus II, #12* (or free atonality)
American Composers of Today, "March of the Puppets" by Sol Berkowitz
American Composers of Today, "Noel Far From Home" by Jan Meyerowitz
American Composers of Today, "Waltz for Brenda" by Roger Sessions
Bartok, Bela   *Fourteen Bagatelles Op. 6* (most of the pieces are expanded tonality) (or advanced level)
Bartok, Bela   *Mikrokosmos, Vol. IV, #114*
°Bartok, Bela   *Mikrokosmos, Vol. IV, #115* ("Bulgarian Rhythm")
Contemporary Collection, Revised Edition, "Procession" by Norman Auerbach
Fiala, George   *Ten Postludes,* II
Fiala, George   *Ten Postludes,* III
Fiala, George   *Ten Postludes,* VIII
°Hindemith, Paul   *Easy Five-Tone Pieces, #8* (some pieces are free atonality)
Lloyd, Norman   *Episodes for Piano, #1*
Lloyd, Norman   *Episodes for Piano, #2*

Starer, Robert   *Seven Vignettes*, II ("Song Without Words")
Starer, Robert   *Seven Vignettes*, IV ("The Interrupted Waltz")
Starer, Robert   *Seven Vignettes*, V ("Chorale")
Starer, Robert   *Seven Vignettes*, VII ("Toccata")
Starer, Robert   *Sketches in Color*, #7 ("Crimson")
Studies in 20th Century Idioms, "Ostinette" by F.R.C. Clarke
°Toch, Ernst   *Echoes from a Small Town Op. 49*, #4
Toch, Ernst   *Echoes from a Small Town Op. 49*, #11
Toch, Ernst   *Reflections Op. 86*, #1
Toch, Ernst   *Reflections Op. 86*, #3
Toch, Ernst   *Reflections Op. 86*, #4
Toch, Ernst   *Three Little Dances Op. 85*, #3 (or free atonality)

ADVANCED

Chavez, Carlos   *Sonatina*
Hindemith, Paul   *Ludus Tonalis*
Lloyd, Norman   *Episodes for Piano*, #3
°Piston, Walter   *Passacaglia*
Szymanowski, Karol   *Mazurkas Op. 50, Book 1*

DIFFICULT

Copland, Aaron   *Passacaglia*

Example 195
BARTOK
Mikrokosmos, Vol. IV, #115
("Bulgarian Rhythm")
(m. 21-32)

Example 196
HINDEMITH
Easy Five-Tone Pieces, # 8
(m. 1-7; 21-27)

Excerpts from *Easy Five-Tone Pieces* by PAUL HINDEMITH. Permission for use authorized by Belwin-Mills Publishing Corporation, exclusive U.S. agents for Schott and Company.

Example 197
TOCH
Echoes from a Small Town
Op. 49, # 4
(m. 26-36)

Excerpt from *Echoes from a Small Town* Op. 49 by ERNST TOCH. Permission for use authorized by Belwin-Mills Publishing Corporation, exclusive U.S. agents for Schott and Company.

Example 198
PISTON
Passacaglia
(m. 1-15; 77-83)

Atonality (free and serial)

The term *atonality* is shrouded with a cloud of controversy and confusion. Literally, it means "without tonality" but many composers and theorists find the description inaccurate for the music that bears this label. It is not the writer's purpose to probe this issue, for whatever the term, the technic still exists. (A rather comprehensive analysis of the problem is given by Otto Deri in Chapter 4 of his book, *Exploring Twentieth-Century Music*.)

There are two types of atonality—*free* and *serial*. Both are based upon the twelve-note dodecuple scale where all tones have equal status; that is, no tone functions as a gravitational point of rest. So in the traditional sense, *no tonal center* is present. The two technics differ only in the area of organization of tones. *Free* contains *no* organization, *serial* does. Both were developed by Arnold Schoenberg in the early twentieth century. Embracing chromatic harmony, he sought a new style that used all twelve tones but which did not have a tonal basis. The result was *free atonality*. The *6 Kleine Klavierstucke Op. 19 (6 Little Piano Pieces Op. 19)* are a product of this stage of his composition.

Example 199
SCHOENBERG
6 Kleine Klavierstucke
Op. 19, IV
(m. 8-14)

Excerpt from *6 Kleine Klavierstucke Op. 19* by ARNOLD SCHOENBERG. ' Copyright 1913 by Universal Edition. Copyright renewed 1940 by Arnold Schoenberg. Used by Permission of Belmont Music Publishers, Los Angeles, California 90049.

But the lack of heirarchy and organization in this system eventually led him to form the highly sophisticated and orderly *serial* technic which has since been widely adopted by many composers. As noted earlier, this kind of writing is based on a *tone row*. Originally this system was called the *twelve-tone serial* technic because all twelve tones were contained in the row. However, tone rows can be of varying lengths. Stravinsky used a five-note row in the "Prelude" of *In Memoriam Dylan Thomas*, and Gunther Schuller employed a long thirty five-note row as an ostinato in "Little Blue Devil" from *Seven Studies on Themes of Paul Klee*.

Example 200
STRAVINSKY
*In Memoriam
Dylan Thomas*
"Dirge-Canons"
("Prelude")
(m. 1-5)

Excerpt from "Dirge-Canons" from *In Memoriam Dylan Thomas* by IGOR STRAVINSKY. ' Copyright 1954 by Boosey & Hawkes, Inc., Reprinted by Permission.

35-note row extracted from *Seven Studies on Themes by Paul Klee*, "Little Blue Devil" by Gunther Schuller.

Example 201
SCHULLER
35-note row

The procedure of serial technic was explained and illustrated in Chapter 1. Briefly, it is this—a composer chooses the number and order of his tones and then adheres to that order, using them up vertically in chords or horizontally. When all the tones are used, either the row is repeated or a transformation is employed. This process continues throughout the work. Some composers are less strict than others about following the row exactly, so modifications are common and should not perplex the conscientious analyst.

The following list contains *free* and *serial* pieces. They are more difficult to decipher than those included in Chapter 1, but the time spent will be valuable to the one who desires a thorough comprehension of the subject.

Examples of Free and Serial Atonality

ELEMENTARY

Adventures in Time and Space, Vol. 1, "Coming and Going" by Mary Mageau (serial)

Kraehenbuehl, David   *Calendar Scenes* (hybrid serial)

INTERMEDIATE

American Composers of Today, "Above, Below and Between" by Robert Starer (free)

American Composers of Today, "Duet" by Milton Babbitt (serial)

American Composers of Today, "Night Song" by Norman Dello Joio (free)

American Composers of Today, "Starscape" by Robert Helps (free)

°Bartok, Bela   *Mikrokosmos, Vol. III*, #91 ("Chromatic Invention") (free)

Contemporary Collection, Revised Edition, "Night Shadows" by Ihor Bilohrud (serial)

°Finney, Ross Lee   *24 Piano Inventions*, #4 ("Barcarolle") (serial)

Hindemith, Paul   *Easy Five-Tone Pieces* (free; expanded tonality)

°Lloyd, Norman   *Episodes for Piano*, #4 (free)

Pentland, Barbara   *Hands Across the C*, #1 ("Sparks") (serial)

Pentland, Barbara   *Hands Across the C*, #2 ("Mists") (serial)

Pentland, Barbara   *Space Studies*, I ("Frolic") (free)

Pentland, Barbara   *Space Studies*, II ("From Outer Space") (free)

Pentland, Barbara   *Space Studies*, IV ("Balancing Act") (free)

Schuman, William   *Three Piano Moods*, "Pensive" (free)

°Starer, Robert   *Seven Vignettes*, III ("Jig-Saw") (serial)

Toch, Ernst   *Echoes from a Small Town Op. 49, #9*
Toch, Ernst   *Echoes from a Small Town Op. 49, #12*
Toch, Ernst   *Echoes from a Small Town Op. 49, #13 (free)*
Toch, Ernst   *Reflections Op. 86, #2 (free)*
°Toch, Ernst   *Three Little Dances Op. 85, #3 (free)*

ADVANCED

Horizons, Book 2, "If" by S. Dolin
Schoenberg, Arnold   *Klavierstucke Op. 33a (serial)*
Schoenberg, Arnold   *Suite für Klavier Op. 25 (serial)*
Webern, Anton   *Variations Op. 27 (serial)*

DIFFICULT

New Music for the Piano (free and serial; expanded tonality)

Example 202
BARTOK
*Mikrokosmos, Vol. III,
#91
("Chromatic Invention")*
(m. 10-17)

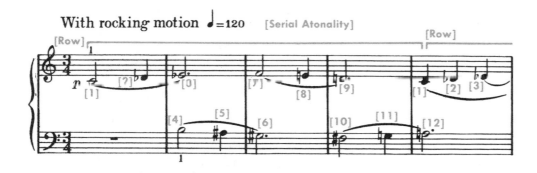

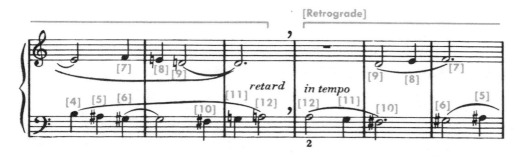

Example 203
FINNEY
*24 Piano Inventions, #4
("Barcarolle")*
(m. 1-11)

Example 204
LLOYD
Episodes for Piano, # 4
(m. 9-18)

Example 205
STARER
Seven Vignettes, III
("Jig-Saw")
(m. 1-8)

Example 206
TOCH
Three Little Dances
Op. 85, # 3
(m. 1-4)

1. Play and study a representative sampling of the piano pieces listed.

2. For additional resource reading, consult the following:

    Austin   *Music in the 20th Century*
    Dallin   *Techniques of Twentieth Century Composition,* Chapters 8 and 14.
    Deri   *Exploring Twentieth-Century Music*
    Hansen   *An Introduction to Twentieth Century Music*
    Hindemith   *A Composer's World*
    Leibowitz   *Schoenberg and His School*
    Machlis   *Introduction to Contemporary Music*
    Marquis   *Twentieth Century Music Idioms*
    Perle   *Serial Composition and Atonality*
    Reti   *Tonality in Modern Music*
    Salzman   *Twentieth-Century Music: An Introduction*
    Stevens   *The Life and Music of Bela Bartok*
    Stravinsky   *Igor Stravinsky: An Autobiography*
    Ward   *Examples for the Study of Musical Style*

3. Do an in-depth study of one of these composers and his musical style: Bartok, Hindemith, Schoenberg or Stravinsky.

4. Listen to the following complete works, with score if possible:

    Britten   *Ceremony of Carols* (modality)
    Copland   *Appalachian Spring* (pandiatonicism; linear polychords; fourths)
    Dallapiccola   *Due Pezzi (Two Pieces) for Orchestra* (twelve-tone)
    Milhaud   *Saudades do Brazil* for piano (polytonality)
    Prokofiev   *Classical Symphony,* First and Second Movements (shifted tonality)
    Schoenberg   *Suite for Piano Op. 25* (twelve-tone)
    Shostakovitch   *Symphony No. 5,* Second Movement (shifted tonality)
    Stravinsky   *In Memoriam Dylan Thomas,* "Dirge-Canons" ("Prelude")
    Stravinsky   *Petrouchka* (pandiatonicism)
    Webern   *Variations for Orchestra Op. 30* (serial)

5. Write a humorous piece using "wrong" notes and shifted tonality.

6. After listening to Milhaud's *Saudades do Brazil,* write a polytonal piano piece.

7. Trace the five-tone row throughout Stravinsky's "Dirge-Canons" ("Prelude") from *In Memoriam Dylan Thomas.*

8. Schoenberg's *Suite for Piano Op. 25* is based upon this tone row of twelve pitches: E, F, G, D♭, G♭, E♭, A♭, D, B, C, A, B♭. Trace this row through several pages of the "Praeludium" or "Gavotte." (You will need to write out the transformations before you begin.) Now, take the same tone row and write your own piece in Gigue style using 6/8 meter.

9. For organists, or those already acquainted with Olivier Messiaen's complex and unique style, read his book *The Technique of My Musical Language* and then listen to and study several of his works, such as:

> *La Nativite du Seigneur* (nine meditations for organ)
> *Les Corps Glorieux,* (especially the third vision, polymodality using original synthetic modes)
> *Hymne* (for large orchestra)
> *L'Ascension (The Ascension: Four Symphonic Meditations)*
> *Turangalila Symphony*

Chapter 5

Texture

Texture in music is the arrangement or combination of the various parts and may be spoken of as being *melodic, chordal* or even *rhythmic; dense* or *thin* depending upon how many lines there are and their proximity to each other. *Monophony* is the term that designates a single melody, as in Gregorian chant; *homophony* refers to a melody accompanied by chords, giving to the score a more harmonic or vertical "look." Most of the music of the classic and romantic periods exemplifies this texture. *Polyphony* is a linear texture wherein two or more independent melodies sound simultaneously. This contrapuntal style reached a high degree of perfection in the Renaissance period, sometimes called the "golden age of polyphony," by such composers as Palestrina and Lassus, but it was Johann Sebastian Bach in the early eighteenth century who carried it to its greatest height. This same polyphonic texture has become idiomatic in much contemporary music.

This chapter, then, will deal with modern polyphony and the various contrapuntal procedures contained therein; also, with unison writing, widely spaced sonorities and extreme registers, pointillism and fragmentation.

Modern polyphony has been stripped of such controls as consonant intervals permissible only on strong beats and allows for any intervals to be prominent. This texture is called *dissonant counterpoint* and is idiomatic in contrapuntal forms. It is also employed liberally in other compositions including those forms that are nameless due to their free, improvisatory construction.

Examples of Dissonant Counterpoint

INTERMEDIATE

Bartok, Bela   *Mikrokosmos, Vol. III*, #91 ("Chromatic Invention")
Bartok, Bela   *Mikrokosmos, Vol. IV*, #106
Bartok, Bela   *Mikrokosmos, Vol. IV*, #109 ("From the Island of Bali")
Bartok, Bela   *Mikrokosmos, Vol. IV*, #114
Bartok, Bela   *Mikrokosmos, Vol. IV*, #117
Bartok, Bela   *Mikrokosmos, Vol. IV*, #121
Diamond, David   *Alone at the Piano, Book 2*, #3
Hindemith, Paul   *Easy Five-Tone Pieces*
°Stravinsky, Soulima   *Three Inventions*, #1 (all three have dissonant counterpoint)

ADVANCED

Hindemith, Paul   *Ludus Tonalis*
Piston, Walter   *Passacaglia*
Riegger, Wallingford   *New and Old*, #8 ("Chromatic")
°Riegger, Wallingford   *New and Old*, #9 ("Dissonant Counterpoint")
°Stevens, Halsey   *Seventeen Piano Pieces*, "Invention"

Example 207
STRAVINSKY, S.
***Three Inventions*, #1**
(m. 1-12)

Example 208
RIEGGER
New and Old, #9
("Dissonant
Counterpoint")
(m. 1-13)

Excerpt from *New and Old* by WALLINGFORD RIEGGER. ˙ Copyright 1947 by Boosey & Hawkes, Inc., Renewed 1974. Reprinted by Permission.

Example 209
STEVENS
Seventeen Piano Pieces
"Invention"
(m. 1-8)

Excerpt from *Seventeen Piano Pieces* by HALSEY STEVENS. ˙ Copyright 1968 by Westwood Press, Inc., copyright transferred to Halsey Stevens, 1971; published by Editio Helios. Reprinted by Permission.

Contrapuntal Procedures

Along with polyphony, modern composers have recalled the contrapuntal procedures of the past. These are *imitation, inversion, diminution, augmentation, variation, canon* and *invertible counterpoint. Mirror writing* is a more recent technic particularly suited to dodecuple music.

Example 210
Contrapuntal Procedures

Examples of Contrapuntal Procedures

1. Imitation

ELEMENTARY

°Adler, Samuel   *Gradus I*, #1
Bartok, Bela   *Mikrokosmos, Vol. II*, #64a and b

INTERMEDIATE

Bartok, Bela   *Mikrokosmos, Vol. IV*, #114

ADVANCED

Bartok, Bela   *Mikrokosmos, Vol. VI*, #145 a and b (b is the inversion of
a with hands switched around)
Riegger, Wallingford   *New and Old*, #8 ("Chromatic")

2. Inversion

INTERMEDIATE

Schuman, William   *Three Piano Moods*, "Dynamic"

3. Diminution

ELEMENTARY

°Stravinsky, Soulima   *Piano Music for Children, Vol. I*, #7 ("For the
kid next door")

INTERMEDIATE

°Bartok, Bela   *Mikrokosmos, Vol. IV*, #117 ("Bourrée")
°Bartok, Bela   *Mikrokosmos, Vol. V*, #124 ("Staccato")
°Stravinsky, Soulima   *Six Sonatinas*, "Sonatina Quinta," First
Movement

ADVANCED

Kabalevsky, Dmitri   *24 Preludes Op. 38*, #24

4. Augmentation

ELEMENTARY

Adler, Samuel   *Gradus I*, #6
Adventures in Time and Space, Vol. I, "Canonic Play" by Lynn
Freeman Olson
Adventures in Time and Space, Vol. I, "Etude" by Ernst Toch
Bartok, Bela   *For Children, Vol. I*, #29
Bartok, Bela   *Mikrokosmos, Vol. II*, #57
Bartok, Bela   *Mikrokosmos, Vol. II*, #60
Frackenpohl, Arthur   *Circus Parade*, #7 ("Follow the Leader")
Stravinsky, Soulima   *Piano Music for Children, Vol. I*, #7 ("For the
kid next door")
Stravinsky, Soulima   *Piano Music for Children, Vol. I*, #17 ("Follow
the leader")

INTERMEDIATE

Adler, Samuel   *Gradus II*, #5
Bartok, Bela   *Mikrokosmos, Vol. III*, #91 ("Chromatic Invention")
Bartok, Bela   *Mikrokosmos, Vol. IV*, #112
Bartok, Bela   *Mikrokosmos, Vol. IV*, #118
Bartok, Bela   *Mikrokosmos, Vol. V*, #123
Bartok, Bela   *Mikrokosmos, Vol. V*, #128
Bartok, Bela   *Mikrokosmos, Vol. V*, #129
Fennimore, Joseph   *Bits and Pieces*, "Canon and Cannon"
°Fletcher, Stanley   *Street Scenes*, "My Shadow Does What I Do"
Hindemith, Paul   *Easy Five-Tone Pieces*, #10
Kubik, Gail   *Sonatina for Piano*, Third Movement
Persichetti, Vincent   *Piano Sonatina No. 2*
°Siegmeister, Elie   *American Kaleidoscope*, "Follow the Leader"
Starer, Robert   *Seven Vignettes*, III ("Jig-Saw")

ADVANCED

°Bernstein, Leonard   *Four Anniversaries*, "For David Diamond"

5. Canon

6. Invertible Counterpoint

INTERMEDIATE
Bartok, Bela   *Mikrokosmos, Vol. IV,* #114
°Hindemith, Paul   *Easy Five-Tone Pieces,* #9
Hindemith, Paul   *Easy Five-Tone Pieces,* #12

ADVANCED
Riegger, Wallingford   *New and Old,* #8 ("Chromatic")

7. Mirror Writing (Reflection)

ELEMENTARY
Adler, Samuel   *Gradus I,* #2
Adler, Samuel   *Gradus I,* #17
Adler, Samuel   *Gradus I,* #18
Adler, Samuel   *Gradus I,* #19
Adventures in Time and Space, Vol. I, "Reflecting" by Lynn Freeman Olson
Dello Joio, Norman   *Suite for the Young,* #2 ("Invention")
Finney, Ross Lee   *32 Piano Games,* II ("Five Fingers")
Finney, Ross Lee   *32 Piano Games,* III ("Thirds")
Finney, Ross Lee   *32 Piano Games,* VII ("Broken Thirds and 3 White-Note Clusters")
°Finney, Ross Lee   *32 Piano Games,* XIII ("Mirror Mimic")

INTERMEDIATE
American Composers of Today, "Chorale" by Lou Harrison
Bartok, Bela   *Mikrokosmos, Vol. IV,* #105
°Bartok, Bela   *Mikrokosmos, Vol. IV,* #109 ("From the Island of Bali")
Bartok, Bela   *Mikrokosmos, Vol. IV,* #120
Contemporary Collection, Revised Edition, "Fanfares" by Gerald Shapiro
Contemporary Collection, Revised Edition, "Magic Circles" by Jean E. Ivey
Contemporary Collection, Revised Edition, "The Mirror" by William Pottebaum
Contemporary Piano Literature, Book 4, "Reflections" by Ross Lee Finney
Contemporary Piano Literature, Book 5-6, "Mirrors" by Ross Lee Finney
Finney, Ross Lee   *24 Piano Inventions,* #4 ("Barcarolle")
Finney, Ross Lee   *24 Piano Inventions,* #8 ("Almost Opposite")
Finney, Ross Lee   *24 Piano Inventions,* #13 ("March")
Finney, Ross Lee   *24 Piano Inventions,* #19 ("Holiday")
Finney, Ross Lee   *24 Piano Inventions,* #20 ("Double Mirrors")
°Finney, Ross Lee   *32 Piano Games,* XXVII ("Mirror Waltz")
°Fletcher, Stanley   *Street Scenes,* "Make Faces at Yourself in the Window"
Lloyd, Norman   *Episodes for Piano,* #1
Pentland, Barbara   *Hands Across the C* ("Stretches 2" is mirror of "Stretches 1")
Schuman, William   *Three Piano Moods,* "Dynamic"

Very calm

Example 211
ADLER
Gradus I, #1
(m. 1-4)

[Inversion]

Excerpt from #1 from *Gradus I* by SAMUEL ADLER.   Copyright 1971 by Oxford University Press, Inc. Reprinted by Permission.

Excerpt from *Piano Music for Children, Vol. I* by SOULIMA STRAVINSKY (P 6127). ' Copyright 1960 by C. F. Peters Corporation, 373 Park Avenue South, New York, New York 10016. Reprint permission granted by the publisher.

Example 212
STRAVINSKY, S.
Piano Music for Children,
Vol. I, # 7
("For the kid next door")
(m. 1-17)

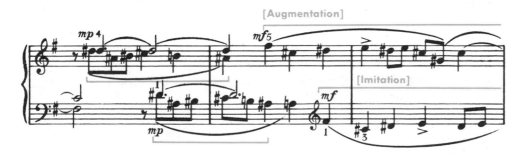

Excerpt from *Mikrokosmos, Vol. IV* by BELA BARTOK. ' Copyright 1940 by Hawkes & Son (London) Ltd., Renewed 1967. Reprinted by Permission of Boosey & Hawkes, Inc.

Example 213
BARTOK
Mikrokosmos,
Vol. IV, # 117
("Bourrée")
(m. 8-14)

Example 214
BARTOK
Mikrokosmos, Vol. V,
#124
("Staccato")
(m. 24-32)

Example 215
STRAVINSKY, S.
Six Sonatinas
"Sonatina Quinta"
First Movement
(m. 17-32)

Not fast, not loud [Canon]

Example 216
FLETCHER
Street Scenes
"My Shadow Does What I Do"
(m. 1-10)

Gaily, crisply [Canon]

Example 217
SIEGMEISTER
American Kaleidoscope
"Follow the Leader"
(m. 1-6)

[Canon]

Example 218
BERNSTEIN
Four Anniversaries
"For David Diamond"
(m. 19-28)

Example 219
HINDEMITH
Easy Five-Tone
Pieces, #9
(m. 1-5)

Langsam, ruhig schreitend

Example 220
FINNEY
32 Piano Games, XIII
("Mirror Mimic")
(m. 1-6)

First way ♩=152   [Mirror]

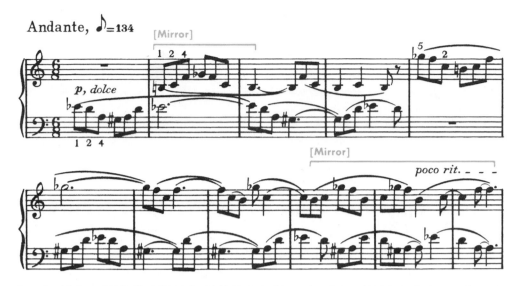

Andante, ♪=134

[Mirror]

Example 221
BARTOK
Mikrokosmos, Vol. IV,
#109
**("From the Island of
Bali")**
(m. 1-11)

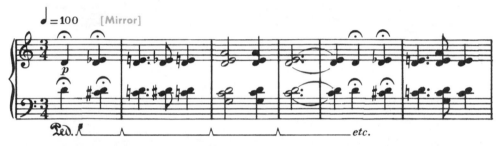

♩=100 [Mirror]

Example 222
FINNEY
32 Piano Games, XXVII
("Mirror Waltz")
(m. 1-6)

With fun, comically [Mirror]

Example 223
FLETCHER
Street Scenes
**"Make Faces at Yourself
in the Window"**
(m. 1-4)

Unison Writing

Unison writing is the doubling of a melody at the octave. It differs from conventional doubling in that the two lines are two or more octaves apart, in different registers, producing a thin, archaic effect akin to ancient monophony. Because of its simple technical demands, composers have found it to be a useful device for elementary piano pieces though it is not restricted to such.

**Examples of Unison
Writing**

ELEMENTARY
Kabalevsky, Dmitri   *24 Little Pieces for Children Op. 39, #8*
°Kabalevsky, Dmitri   *24 Little Pieces for Children Op. 39, #11*

INTERMEDIATE
°Bartok, Bela   *Mikrokosmos, Vol. III, #77* ("Little Study")
Bartok, Bela   *Mikrokosmos, Vol. III, #92*
°Bartok, Bela   *Mikrokosmos, Vol. IV, #98* ("Thumb Under")
Pinto, Octavio   *Scenas Infantis, #2* ("Ring Around the Rosy")

ADVANCED
Bartok, Bela   *Fourteen Bagatelles Op. 6, #9*
Harris, Roy   *Toccata*
°*New Music for the Piano,* "Allegro on a Pakistan Lute Tune" by Alan
Hovhaness

**Example 224
KABALEVSKY
24 Little Pieces for
Children Op. 39, #11**
(m. 1-7)

Excerpt from *24 Little Pieces for Children Op. 39* by DMITRI KABALEVSKY. Reprinted by Permission of International Music Company.

**Example 225
BARTOK
Mikrokosmos,
Vol. III, #77
("Little Study")**
(m. 1-4)

Excerpt from *Mikrokosmos, Vol. III* by BELA BARTOK. ° Copyright 1940 by Hawkes & Son (London) Ltd., Renewed 1967. Reprinted by Permission of Boosey & Hawkes, Inc.

**Example 226
BARTOK
Mikrokosmos,
Vol. IV, #98
("Thumb Under")**
(m. 1-13)

Excerpt from *Mikrokosmos, Vol. IV* by BELA BARTOK. ° Copyright 1940 by Hawkes & Son (London) Ltd., Renewed 1967. Reprinted by Permission of Boosey & Hawkes, Inc.

Excerpt from *Allegro on a Pakistan Lute Tune* by ALAN HOVHANESS. Reprinted from *New Music for the Piano.* Copyright by Lawson-Gould Music Publishers, Inc., New York, N.Y. Used by Permission.

Example 227
HOVHANESS
*Allegro on a Pakistan
Lute Tune*
(m. 1-5)

Widely Spaced Sonorities and Extreme Registers

As noted earlier, music of the tonal period can usually be reduced to four parts—soprano, alto, tenor and bass. The various tones at any given time are distributed across the span of these ranges which would be roughly the distance of four to five octaves. Contemporary composers have extended this distance, using the entire gamut of the keyboard in piano music. Both hands may be very high or very low. When they are widely separated, the middle register may be filled in or left silent, as in the case of unison writing.

Examples of Widely Spaced Sonorities and Extreme Registers

ELEMENTARY
°Finney, Ross Lee *32 Piano Games,* VIII ("Everything Everywhere")
Finney, Ross Lee *32 Piano Games,* XVII ("Up and Down")

INTERMEDIATE
°*American Composers of Today,* "Night Song" by Norman Dello Joio
°*American Composers of Today,* "Starscape" by Robert Helps
Finney, Ross Lee *32 Piano Games,* XI ("3 White-Note Clusters, High and Low")
Finney, Ross Lee *32 Piano Games,* XXXII ("Winter")
°Ginastera, Alberto *12 American Preludes, Vol. I,* #12 ("In the first Pentatonic Major Mode")
Krenek, Ernst *12 Short Piano Pieces Op. 83,* #10 ("On the High Mountains")
°Prokofiev, Serge *Children's Pieces Op. 65,* #1 ("Morning")
Prokofiev, Serge *Children's Pieces Op. 65,* #5 ("Regrets")
Prokofiev, Serge *Children's Pieces Op. 65,* #8 ("The Rain and the Rainbow")

ADVANCED
Bartok, Bela *Three Rondos,* II
Bartok, Bela *Three Rondos,* III

DIFFICULT
Rorem, Ned *Toccata*

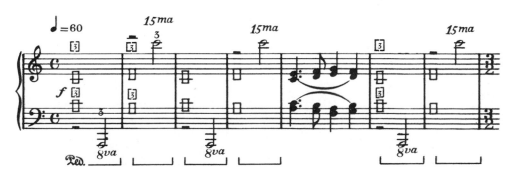

Excerpt from *32 Piano Games* by ROSS LEE FINNEY (P 66256). ' Copyright 1969 by Henmar Press, Inc., 373 Park Avenue South, New York, New York 10016. Reprint permissioned granted by the publisher.

Example 228
FINNEY
32 Piano Games, VIII
("Everything
Everywhere")
(m. 1-7)

Texture   147

Example 229
DELLO JOIO
Night Song
(m. 1-4)

Example 230
HELPS
Starscape
(m. 5-9)

Example 231
GINASTERA
12 American Preludes,
Vol. I, #12
("In the first Pentatonic
Major Mode")
(m. 22-23)

Example 232
PROKOFIEV
*Children's Pieces
Op. 65, #1
("Morning")*
(m. 1-6)

Excerpt from *Children's Pieces Op. 65* by SERGE PROKOFIEV. Used by Permission of Edwin F. Kalmus.

Pointillism is a fragmentary style in which continuous solid lines and textures are avoided. It is a twelve-tone device imitative of the pointillist school of painting where a design is created on canvas by multi-colored dots. Other forms of fragmentation exist and are recognizable by blotches of sound punctuated by frequent rests.

Pointillism and Fragmentation

Example 233
Pointillism

Examples of Pointillism

ELEMENTARY
  Adventures in Time and Space, Vol. I, "Count Down—Blast Off" by
  Ann Riley

INTERMEDIATE
  °Adler, Samuel *Gradus II,* #8a and b
  °Finney, Ross Lee *24 Piano Inventions,* #12 ("Doubt")
  Krenek, Ernst *12 Short Piano Pieces Op. 83,* #8 ("Glass Figures")
  Pentland, Barbara *Hands Across the C*
  Pentland, Barbara *Space Studies,* I ("Frolic")
  Pentland, Barbara *Space Studies,* IV ("Balancing Act")
  Schuman, William *Three Piano Moods,* "Pensive"

ADVANCED
  New Music for the Piano, "Two Episodes: 1933," I by Arthur Berger
  °Webern, Anton *Variations Op. 27,* III

DIFFICULT
  New Music for the Piano, "Partitions" by Milton Babbitt

Example 234
ADLER
Gradus II, #8b
(m. 1-5)

Excerpt from #8 from *Gradus II* by SAMUEL ADLER. ⁵ Copyright 1971 by Oxford University Press, Inc. Reprinted by Permission.

Example 235
FINNEY
24 Piano Inventions, #12
("Doubt")
(m. 1-4)

Excerpt from *24 Piano Inventions* by ROSS LEE FINNEY (P 66262). ⁵ Copyright 1971 by Henmar Press, Inc., 373 Park Avenue South, New York, New York 10016.
Reprint permission granted by the publisher.

Example 236
WEBERN
Variations Op. 27, III
(m. 50-53)

Excerpt from *Variations Op. 27* by ANTON WEBERN. ⁵ Copyright 1937 by Universal Edition A.G., Wien, Renewal 1965. Used by Permission.

Examples of
Fragmentation

ELEMENTARY
Dello Joio, Norman   *Suite for the Young, #6* ("Echoes")

INTERMEDIATE
°*American Composers of Today*, "Prelude" by William Sydeman
Diamond, David   *Alone at the Piano, Book 2, #5*
Diamond, David   *Alone at the Piano, Book 2, #6*
Diamond, David   *Alone at the Piano, Book 2, #7*
°Krenek, Ernst   *12 Short Piano Pieces Op. 83, #5* ("Little Chessmen")
Krenek, Ernst   *12 Short Piano Pieces Op. 83, #11* ("Bells in the Fog")
Krenek, Ernst   *12 Short Piano Pieces Op. 83, #12* ("Indian-Summer
Day")
°Schoenberg, Arnold   *6 Kleine Klavierstucke Op. 19, II*

Example 237
SYDEMAN
Prelude
(m. 1-7)

Example 238
KRENEK
12 Short Piano Pieces
Op. 83, #5
("Little Chessmen")
(m. 1-5)

Example 239
SCHOENBERG
6 Kleine Klavierstucke
Op. 19, II
(m. 7-9)

Suggested Assignments

1. Play and study a representative sampling of the piano pieces listed.

2. For additional resource reading, consult the following:

   Dallin   *Techniques of Twentieth Century Composition*, Chapter 13.
   Searle   *Twentieth-Century Counterpoint*

3. Listen to the following complete works, with score if possible:

   Bartok   *String Quartet No. 4*, First and Fifth Movements (inversion; mirror; canon)
   Carter   *Eight Etudes and a Fantasy for Woodwind Quartet*, "Etude No. 7" (This is all on one pitch, concert G.)
   Hindemith   *Ludus Tonalis* for piano (dissonant counterpoint)
   Honegger   *Symphony No. 5*, First Movement (thick, polychordal opening changing to a thin, linear texture for middle section. Notice how texture becomes an ingredient of form in this work.)
   Penderecki   *Passion According to St. Luke* (sound mass)
   Penderecki   *Threnody for the Victims of Hiroshima* (solid mass of sound including quarter tones and glissandos)
   Vaughn Williams   *Symphony No. 6 in E Minor* (polyphonic)

4. Play through *New Music for the Piano*, selected by Joseph Prostakoff. (Most of the pieces are serial.)

5. Using a pointillistic or fragmented texture, construct several phrases in free or serial atonality.

6. Write a two-part invention in free atonality using dissonant counterpoint. Be sure to include imitative devices, such as mirror, imitation, inversion, etc.

7. Write a short piece in A B A form in which a dense, harmonic texture is contrasted with a thin, linear one.

8. Write a canon for two instruments. (For a model, listen to or play Franck's *Violin—Piano Sonata*, Last Movement, or play the Third Movement of Kubik's *Sonatina for Piano*.)

9. Using Example 231 as a model, compose a grandiose piano piece whose range and texture cover the keyboard. Keep the difficulty within your own playing ability.

Chapter 6
Form

Introduction

This chapter deals with the formal innovations of the twentieth century, for an understanding of the over-all plan of a work is essential to its total comprehension and successful performance. Only those features which are commonly found in preparatory piano literature will be emphasized, allowing the reader to pursue the subject of form in greater depth at a later time.

Composers have not abandoned forms of the past but have either duplicated or modified them. Modification often means shortening, for many composers have shunned the verbosity of the late romantic period, preferring rather to shape their ideas more succinctly. Themes are terse, sometimes only a motive in length, and literal repetition is rare. The recurrence of an idea is either condensed or varied.

Another area of modification is tonality. This was the primary ingredient for building the large formal structures of the past—i.e., binary, ternary, rondo, minuet and trio, sonata-allegro, as well as fugue and other contrapuntal forms. For, once the principle of a strong key center was established, *modulation*—the movement fron one key to another—became inevitable and paved the way for the sectioning of these forms. But with the gradual breakdown of tonality toward the end of the nineteenth century came the need for shortened forms and new ingredients to hold the longer ones together. Works were based *on* a key rather than *in* a key. In the absence of a strong gravitational tonal center, such means as texture, tempo, dynamics, rhythm, instrumentation, articulation and range were utilized for the sectioning of large works. In serial music the tone row became the organizational ingredient.

Asymmetric and Irregular-Length Phrases

In spite of these and other changes, one still finds in contemporary music, as in the past, a careful balance of repetition, contrast and variety, activity and repose, ascending and descending motion. For these elements are basic to all artistic musical structures regardless of style-period or idiom.

Aside from the dissolution of tonality, the most dramatic change in music of this century has been in the area of rhythm and meter. In Chapter 2 it was noted that new musical ideas were not always symmetrically constituted to fit the old meters. Consequently, asymmetric meters and changing meters became a necessity to accommodate this new rhythmic freedom. As a further consequence, phrase lengths were affected. Whereas the average phrase in tonal music is four (eight or sixteen) measures, barring extensions, phrases in modern music are often asymmetric (i.e., three, five, seven measures) and/or of irregular lengths. Such unpredictable, interior construction of a piece must be perceived by the performer if correct phrasing is to be achieved. As punctuation is to prose, so phrasing is to music. Comprehension depends on it.

Examples of Asymmetric and Irregular-Length Phrases

ELEMENTARY
°Bartok, Bela   *First Term at the Piano*, #15 ("Wedding Song")
°Stravinsky, Igor   *Les Cinq Doigts (The Five Fingers)*, #1
°Stravinsky, Igor   *Les Cinq Doigts (The Five Fingers)*, #4
Stravinsky, Soulima   *Piano Music for Children, Vol. I*, #1 ("Stepping stones")
Stravinsky, Soulima   *Piano Music for Children, Vol. I*, #2 ("Wandering")
Stravinsky, Soulima   *Piano Music for Children, Vol. I*, #3 ("Swaying")
Stravinsky, Soulima   *Piano Music for Children, Vol. I*, #6 ("Seesaw")
°Stravinsky, Soulima   *Piano Music for Children, Vol. I*, #19 ("Mama and Papa are talking")

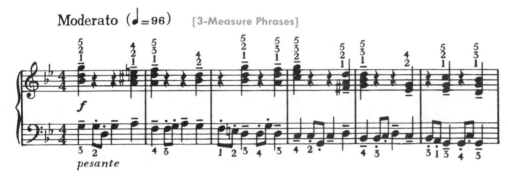

Example 240
BARTOK
First Term at the Piano, # 15
("Wedding Song")
(m. 1-6)

Excerpt from *First Term at the Piano* by BELA BARTOK.   Copyright 1950 by Boosey & Hawkes, Inc. Reprinted by Permission.

Example 241
STRAVINSKY
Les Cinq Doigts, # 1
(m. 1-14)

Excerpt from *Les Cinq Doigts* by IGOR STRAVINSKY. Reprinted with kind permission of J & W Chester/Edition Wilhelm Hansen London Limited.

Example 242
STRAVINSKY
Les Cinq Doigts, #4
(m. 1-8)

Example 243
STRAVINSKY, S.
Piano Music for Children,
Vol. I, #19
("Mama and Papa are
talking")
(m. 1-6)

Example 244
BARTOK
Ten Easy Pieces
"Dance of the Slovaks"
(m. 1-10)

Slowly flowing [Irregular-Length Phrases]

Con moto [3-Measure Phrase]

Example 245
THOMSON
A Day-Dream
(m. 1-11)

Example 246
STRAVINSKY, S.
Six Sonatinas
"Sonatina Quinta"
First Movement
(m. 1-4)

Cadences

Cadences are "breathing" places at the ends of phrases and bring to music either a temporary or final cessation of motion. In the early tonal period they appeared regularly and predictably. Ending on the V chord brought temporary rest; on the I, final repose. Cadences were much less clear during the chromatic era in the late nineteenth century and contributed to the weakening of tonality.

However, a neo-classic school emerged in the early twentieth century, led by Prokofiev and Shostakovitch, and with it came a revival of clearly defined cadences as seen in the following example. (See also Prokofiev's *Classical Symphony*.)

Example 247
PROKOFIEV
Four Pieces Op. 32
"Gavotte"
(m. 1-17)

Excerpt from *Four Pieces Op. 32* by SERGE PROKOFIEV. Used by Permission of Edwin F. Kalmus.

Some composers still honor the traditional V-I but with modifications in the structure of either or both chords. Modal changes are common in the dominant (i.e., lowered third and/or fifth), and the tonic may appear open (no third) or with both major and minor thirds, or with added tones. Usually the final chord is longer and less dissonant than previous ones, thus sounding comparatively restful.

Example 248
SHOSTAKOVITCH
24 Preludes Op. 34, #6
(m. 54-58)

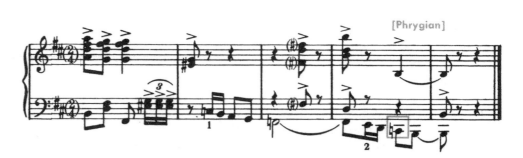

Excerpt from *24 Preludes Op. 34* by DMITRI SHOSTAKOVITCH. Copyright by G. Schirmer, Inc. Used by Permission.

Example 249
STARER
Above, Below and
Between
(m. 61-71)

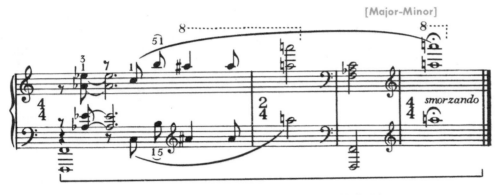

Example 250
SCHUMAN
Three Piano Moods
"Pensive"
(m. 23-26)

Example 251
HINDEMITH
Easy Five-Tone Pieces,
 # 5
(m. 20-25)

Another modification is in the relationship of the last two bass tones which in tonal writing is usually a perfect fourth or perfect fifth. The *third* was popular in Liszt's day and still occurs. But a further departure from tradition is observed in some music where the pivotal point, substituting for the dominant (V) axis, is a *tritone* away from the tonic. In the key of C, this tone is F♯ (or G♭).

Example 252
KHACHATURIAN
Adventures of Ivan, # 4
("Ivan Goes to a Party")
(m. 108-118)

[Third Relationship]

Excerpt from *Adventures of Ivan* by ARAM KHACHATURIAN. Copyright by G. Schirmer, Inc. Used by Permission.

Example 253
MILANO
Toccata
(m. 73-75)

[Tritone]

Excerpt from *Toccata* by ROBERT MILANO. ' Copyright 1963 by Beekman Music, Inc. Used by Permission.

In a polyphonic texture cadences are determined by linear considerations. As in previous eras, contrary motion approaching a cadence is common in dissonant counterpoint, but any interval is regarded a satisfactory axis or stopping point by contemporary composers.

[Dissonant Counterpoint]

Example 254
BABBITT
Duet
(m. 16b-19)

[Tritone]

Excerpt from *Duet* by MILTON BABBITT. Reprinted from *American Composers of Today*. Copyright MCMLVI by Edward B. Marks Music Corporation. All Rights Reserved. International Copyright Secured. Used by Permission.

Atonal cadences are more ambiguous and harder to anticipate aurally. So tempo, texture and dynamics must assume a greater responsibility to compensate for the absence of a gravitational point.

[Atonal]

Excerpt from #10 from *Gradus II* by SAMUEL ADLER. Copyright 1971 by Oxford University Press, Inc. Reprinted by Permission.

Example 255
ADLER
Gradus II, #10
(m. 10-13)

Examples of Cadences

ELEMENTARY
Diamond, David   *Album for the Young*

INTERMEDIATE
°Adler, Samuel   *Gradus II,* #6 (clusters)
°Adler, Samuel   *Gradus II,* #10 (serial; density of last chord) (see Example 255)
°*American Composers of Today,* "Above, Below and Between" by Robert Starer (open fifth) (see Example 249)
°*American Composers of Today,* "Duet" by Milton Babbitt (dissonant counterpoint) (see Example 254)
°*American Composers of Today,* "Prelude" by William Sydeman (atonal)
°Bartok, Bela   *For Children, Vol. II,* #9 (Lydian)
Casella, Alfredo   *11 Children's Pieces*
Contemporary Collection, Revised Edition
°Hindemith, Paul   *Easy Five-Tone Pieces,* #5 ($\frac{5}{4}$ chord; the cadences of all the pieces are noteworthy) (see Example 251)
Kabalevsky, Dmitri   *Children's Pieces Op. 27,* "Sad Little Tale" (Phrygian)
°Khachaturian, Aram   *Adventures of Ivan,* #1 ("Ivan Sings") (Phrygian)
°Khachaturian, Aram   *Adventures of Ivan,* #4 ("Ivan Goes to a Party") (third relationship) (see Example 252)
Khachaturian, Aram   *Adventures of Ivan,* #7 ("Ivan's Hobbyhorse")
°Persichetti, Vincent   *Piano Sonatina No. 4,* Third Movement (Mixolydian)
°Schuman, William   *Three Piano Moods,* "Pensive" (major-minor) (see Example 250)

ADVANCED
Kabalevsky, Dmitri   *24 Preludes Op. 38,* #2 (Dorian)
Kabalevsky, Dmitri   *24 Preludes Op. 38,* #12
Kabalevsky, Dmitri   *24 Preludes Op. 38,* #13 (major-minor)
Kabalevsky, Dmitri   *24 Preludes Op. 38,* #19
Kabalevsky, Dmitri   *24 Preludes Op. 38,* #24
Kennan, Kent   *Three Preludes,* #3 (tritone)
°Milano, Robert   *Toccata* (tritone) (see Example 253)
Milhaud, Darius   *Saudades do Brazil, Book 2,* #8 ("Tijuca") (major-minor) (see Example 107)
°Prokofiev, Serge   *Visions Fugitives Op. 22,* #14 (clusters)
Riegger, Wallingford   *New and Old,* #8 ("Chromatics") (tritone)
°Shostakovitch, Dmitri   *24 Preludes Op. 34,* #6 (Phrygian) (see Example 248)

Example 256
ADLER
Gradus II, #6
(m. 20-23)

Example 257
SYDEMAN
Prelude
(m. 25-30)

Example 258
BARTOK
For Children, Vol. II, #9
(m. 8-14)

Example 259
KHACHATURIAN
Adventures of Ivan, #1
("Ivan Sings")
(m. 27-29)

[Mixolydian]

Excerpt from *Piano Sonatina No. 4* by VINCENT PERSICHETTI. ' Copyright 1957 by Elkan-Vogel, Inc. Used by Permission.

Example 260
PERSICHETTI
Piano Sonatina No. 4
Third Movement
(m. 45-51)

[Clusters]

Excerpt from *Visions Fugitives Op. 22* by SERGE PROKOFIEV. Published MCMXLI by Edward B. Marks Music Corporation.   All Rights Reserved.   Used by Permission.

Example 261
PROKOFIEV
Visions Fugitives Op. 22,
#14
(m. 41-43)

Contrapuntal Forms

The establishment of dissonant counterpoint as a viable twentieth century texture is responsible for the revival of old polyphonic structures, such as the *invention, fugue, chaconne* and *passacaglia*. As expected, composers have adapted these "forms" to the new materials of the present century making change imperative, particularly in the area of tonal relationships. But the basic contrapuntal treatment of ideas is the same as in older music bearing these titles.

For the advanced pianist, Hindemith's *Ludus Tonalis* is the most notable example. It consists of a series of interludes and fugues with the final *Postludium* being a retrograde-inversion (hands reversed) of the opening *Praeludium*. The *24 Preludes and Fugues* of Shostakovitch are a modern equivalent of the *Well-Tempered Clavier* by Johann Sebastian Bach, ranging in difficulty from late intermediate to advanced. The Finney *24 Piano Inventions* are not inventions in the polyphonic sense (so stated at the beginning) and, therefore, are not included in this list of examples.

INTERMEDIATE

Adler, Samuel   *Gradus II,* #11 (in the style of an invention)
Kabalevsky, Dmitri   *6 Preludes and Fugues Op. 61*
Persichetti, Vincent   *Little Piano Book,* #13 ("Fugue")
Scott, Cyril   *Pastoral Suite,* "Passacaglia"
Stravinsky, Soulima   *Three Inventions*

Examples of
Contrapuntal Forms

ADVANCED
 Fuleihan, Anis   *Fugue*
 Harris, Roy   *Toccata* (fugal section)
 Hindemith, Paul   *Ludus Tonalis* (interludes and fugues)
 Piston, Walter   *Passacaglia*
 Shostakovitch, Dmitri   *24 Preludes Op. 34,* #4 (in the style of a fugue)
 Shostakovitch, Dmitri   *24 Preludes and Fugues Op. 87*
 Stevens, Halsey   *Seventeen Piano Pieces,* "Chaconne"
 Stevens, Halsey   *Seventeen Piano Pieces,* "Invention"

DIFFICULT
 Copland, Aaron   *Passacaglia*

Other Forms

Before considering other molds into which contemporary composers have poured their musical offerings, it should be recognized that many works are freely constructed, but this in no way implies that they are without shape. *Alone at the Piano* by David Diamond and *Easy Five-Tone Pieces* by Paul Hindemith are of this kind—a series of phrases. In the case of serial music the tone row becomes the basic structural element.

A glance through the list of piano music included in Appendix E discloses other forms drawn from the past which are presently in vogue—sonata, variation and multi-movement works resembling old dance suites. The framework of the individual movements may be improvisatory, fugal or that of a traditional type, such as song-form, sonata-allegro or rondo. In these latter forms repetition is a salient feature, so one expects to find considerable modification in light of what was mentioned in the Introduction of this chapter—that exact repetition is rare. *Da Capo* signs and repeat marks are sparce. When themes do recur they are usually varied and/or shortened. And, similar to contrapuntal forms, *any* relationship of keys within a work is deemed suitable by modern composers.

When tonality is present, themes are distinguishable from each other by being assigned to different keys. On the other hand, when the tonality is vague or nonexistent, it is rendered useless for the achievement of this task. In such situations, opposing themes must differ intrinsically for easy identification by the listener.

Attributable to Bartok is *arch* form. It is usually in five or seven parts and resembles sonata-allegro form except the themes appear in reverse order in the recapitulation. In the two diagrams which follow, the bracketed letters "C" and "D" represent the development. Due to its proportions, this form is not used in smaller piano works as far as the writer knows.

Example 262
Arch Form

A B [C] B A

or

A B C [D] C B A

In the following list of examples, those identifiable by title in Appendix E are not included.

ELEMENTARY
  Stevens, Everett   *Six Modal Miniatures* (all are ABA)
  Stravinsky, Soulima   *Piano Music for Children, Vol. II,* #24
    ("Mirrors") (theme and variations)

INTERMEDIATE
  °Stravinsky, Soulima   *Six Sonatinas,* "Sonatina Sesta," First
    Movement (theme and variations)
  Stravinsky, Soulima   *Six Sonatinas,* "Sonatina Sesta," Second
    Movement (fughetta)

Tema
Larghetto [Theme and Variations]

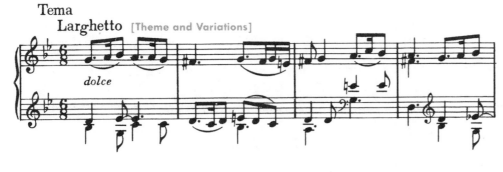

Example 263
STRAVINSKY, S.
Six Sonatinas
"Sonatina Sesta"
First Movement
(m. 1-16)

Var. 1
Poco più mosso

Suggested Assignments

1. Play and study as many different forms as possible which are listed in this chapter and Appendix E.

2. Listen to the following complete works, with score if possible.

> Barber   *Sonata in E Flat Minor Op. 26* (First Movement, sonata allegro; Second Movement, rondo; Third Movement, twelve-tone; Fourth Movement, fugue)
>
> Bartok   *String Quartet No. 4* (Arch Form: First and Fifth Movements are similar; Second and Fourth also similar; Third provides the "arch"; also, cadence of First Movement is major-minor and Phrygian)
>
> Dello Joio   *Sonata No. 3* for piano, First Movement (chant-like theme and variations)
>
> Hindemith   *Sonata No. 2* for piano (Haydnesque in texture and form)
>
> Hindemith   *Sonata No. 3* for piano, Last Movement (fugue)
>
> Prokofiev   *Classical Symphony*
>
> Prokofiev   *Piano Concerto No. 3*, Second Movement (theme and variations)
>
> Schuman, William   *Symphony No. 3* (movements are marked, I Passacaglia, Fugue; II Chorale, Toccata)
>
> Stravinsky   *Symphony of Psalms* for chorus and orchestra, I (E Phrygian melody throughout and Phrygian cadence); II (double fugue)

3. For additional resource reading, consult the following:

> Cone   *Musical Form and Musical Performance*
>
> Dallin   *Techniques of Twentieth Century Composition*, Chapters 9 and 12.
>
> Eschman   *Changing Forms in Modern Music*
>
> Graves   *Twentieth-Century Fugue*

4. Write a few short studies using irregular-length phrases and new cadences.

Chapter 7
Jazz

The years prior to World War I marked the rise of four influential styles which were to dominate the musical scene for half a century—those of Bartok (1881-1945), Stravinsky (1882-1971), Schoenberg (1874-1951) and———Jazz.

Jazz is primarily an instrumental idiom which originated in New Orleans by black musicians, was brought to New York City about 1912 and eventually spread to other major cities throughout the country. Its loud and strident sound is generated by a small group of instruments, usually trumpet, trombone, clarinet, banjo or plucked string bass and drums. (The saxophone was added some time later.) In contrast to the more euphonious blend of a symphony orchestra, the instruments of a jazz band operate more or less independently as though clamoring for attention. Syncopation, "blues" notes, tonic with added sixth, chromatic passing and auxiliary chords, counterpoint and improvisation make up the jazz musical style in which rhythm, melody and tone color are the primary elements.

Usually in duple meter, the off-beat accent characteristic of jazz is dually emphasized by ponderous foot-tapping and the conductor's method of beating all beats down. Polyrhythms, where the eighth notes are regrouped into patterns of three in conflict with the steady metric accent, as well as the cross-rhythms of two-against-three and three-against-four are also common. The ♩. ♪ rhythmic pattern is used frequently in the melody but is performed freely, as in eighteenth century music, rather than mathematically. It is often interrupted by syncopated notes or by a triplet figure. Triplet patterns are also used in the accompaniment as "filler" when there is a break in the melody line.

"Blues" notes, flatted thirds and sevenths, function as expressive coloring (often appoggiaturas) and should *not* be thought of as exact notes on the piano or as forming a new scale. Unlike the piano, the trumpet, trombone, clarinet, saxophone and human voice are all capable of a sliding technic that enables them to produce sounds "in the cracks." *Blues* music is an improvisatory folk song style consisting of a pattern of three four-measure phrases with the simple harmonic foundation of I, IV-I, and V-I. The melody is made up of short phrases inviting antiphonal responses from the other instruments during its frequent rests. When performing *blues* piano music, the solo pianist must learn to imitate this latter and important trait.

Improvisation, the art of "making it up as you go along," is probably the most distinguishing feature of jazz. For jazz is *not* what is seen on the page but what is heard. One learns to perform a jazz piece by hearing it played. Jazz improvisation involves melody, rhythm and tempo, and is carried on over a harmonic skeleton by one soloist or by a group of players.

Ragtime is the jazz adaptation for piano and, therefore, must rely upon written notation. Its typical formal structures are ABCD and ABACD.

Of particular merit for the study of jazz are the publications of John Mehegan listed in the Bibliography. The set of six *Jazz and Blues* books by David Kraehenbuehl in the Frances Clark Library contain pieces on the elementary and intermediate levels, selections from which are recorded by the composer on a 12″ LP.

Books and articles on jazz are listed separately in the Bibliography, Appendix C. Peter Hansen's book, *An Introduction to the Twentieth Century,* deals briefly but significantly with the characteristics of jazz; whereas, William Austin's text, *Music in the 20th Century,* is noteworthy for its two chapters on jazz and exhaustive bibliography.

All the examples included here will contain *some* jazz features, but important characteristics, such as improvisation, will be noticeably absent.

Examples of Jazz

ELEMENTARY

Contemporary Collection, Revised Edition, "Scherzo on Tenth Avenue" by David Kraehenbuehl
°*Contempos in Jade,* "Blue Walk" by Ruth Perdew
°Dello Joio, Norman *Suite for the Young,* #9 ("Small Fry") (blues)
Grove, Roger *Jazz About*
Kraehenbuehl, David *Jazz and Blues, Books 1-3*
Siegmeister, Elie *American Kaleidoscope,* "Banjo Tune"
°Siegmeister, Elie *American Kaleidoscope,* "A Bit of Jazz"
Siegmeister, Elie *American Kaleidoscope,* "Blues"
Siegmeister, Elie *American Kaleidoscope,* "Boogie"
Siegmeister, Elie *American Kaleidoscope,* "Boogie Rhythm"

INTERMEDIATE

Adler, Samuel *Gradus II,* #18
Contemporary Collection, Revised Edition, "Etude in Blue" by David Kraehenbuehl
Fennimore, Joseph *Bits and Pieces,* "Bit of Blues"
Kraehenbuehl, David *Jazz and Blues, Books 4-6*
°Kraehenbuehl, David *Jazz and Blues, Book 5,* "Fade-Out Boogie"
°Starer, Robert *Sketches in Color,* #4 ("Bright Orange")
°Tansman, Alexandre *Pour les Enfants, 4th Set,* #6 ("Disque")

ADVANCED

Barber, Samuel   *Excursions Op. 20* (especially #1 and #2)
Bolcom, William   *Graceful Ghost* (rag)
Bolcom, William   *Three Popular Rags*, "Seabiscuits"
Classic Piano Rags, selected by Rudi Blesh
Davis, Allan   *Razorback Reel*
Gershwin, George   *Preludes for Piano*
Hindemith, Paul   *Suite for Piano "1922" Op. 26*, "Ragtime"
Joplin, Scott   *Collected Piano Works* (many published separately and in easier arrangements, such as "The Entertainer" and "Maple Leaf Rag")
Mehegan, John   *Jazz Preludes*

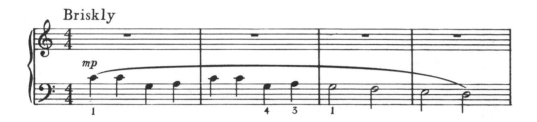

Example 264
PERDEW
Blue Walk
(m. 1-20)

Example 265
DELLO JOIO
Suite for the Young, #9
("Small Fry")
(m. 3-10)

Example 266
SIEGMEISTER
American Kaleidoscope
"A Bit of Jazz"
(m. 13-16)

Example 267
KRAEHENBUEHL
Jazz and Blues, Book 5
"Fade-Out Boogie"
(m. 1-8)

Example 268
STARER
Sketches in Color, #4
(**"Bright Orange"**)
(m. 1-15)

Example 269
TANSMAN
Pour les Enfants, 4th Set,
#6
(**"Disque"**)
(m. 1-7)

Jazz   171

Suggested Assignments

1. Play and study a representative sampling of the piano pieces listed.

2. For additional resource reading, consult the following:

   Austin   *Music in the 20th Century*, Chapters 11 and 15.
   Chase   *America's Music*, Chapters 21 through 24.
   Hansen   *An Introduction to Twentieth Century Music*, Chapter 5.
   (Other books are listed in the separate Jazz Bibliography.)

3. Do a comparative study of Improvisation in the Baroque period and in Jazz.

4. Write a short piano piece in the "blues" style.

5. Listen to as much authentic jazz as possible, live or recorded. For a drill in rhythm and meters, Dave Brubeck's recording, *Adventures in Time,* is recommended.

6. For an example of third-stream jazz, listen to Gunther Schuller's *Seven Studies on Themes of Paul Klee.* The third study, "Little Blue Devil" contains a thirty-five note tone row.

Chapter 8
Innovations

Crucial to accurate reading is the understanding of all notational symbols. In recent years, new symbols have been devised as visual representations of the many innovative effects composers have created.

In her article, "A New Look for New Sounds," Marjory Irvin gives a most comprehensive coverage of this important subject and includes the five charts which are reprinted on the following pages.[10]

---

[10] Marjory Irvin, "A New Look for New Sounds," *Clavier* (April 1973), pp. 15-18.

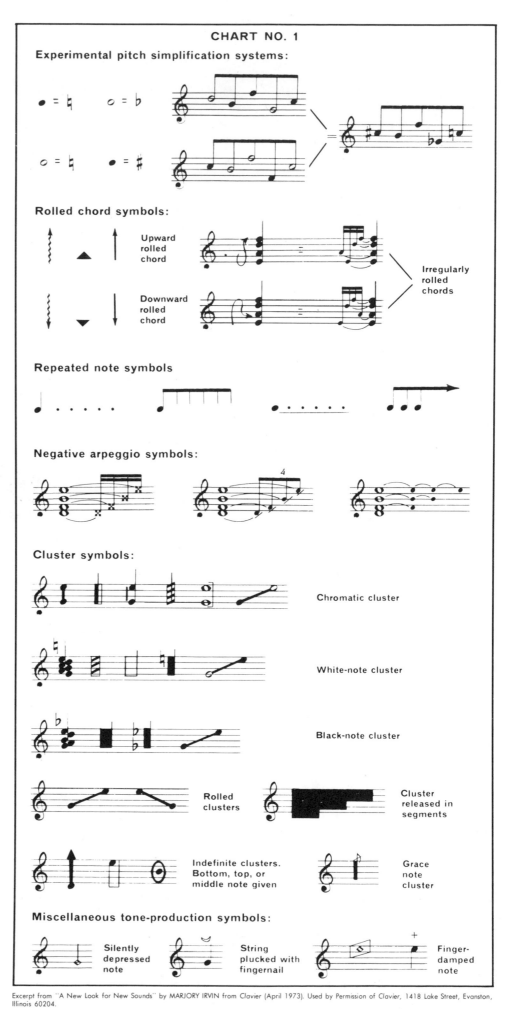

Excerpt from "A New Look for New Sounds" by MARJORY IRVIN from Clavier (April 1973). Used by Permission of Clavier, 1418 Lake Street, Evanston, Illinois 60204.

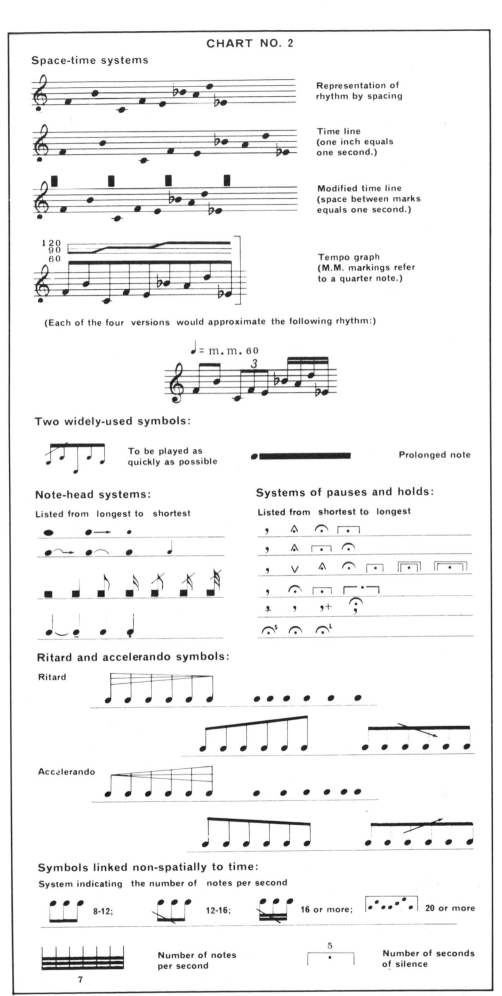

CHART NO. 2

Space-time systems

Representation of rhythm by spacing

Time line (one inch equals one second.)

Modified time line (space between marks equals one second.)

Tempo graph (M.M. markings refer to a quarter note.)

(Each of the four versions would approximate the following rhythm:)

♩ = m. m. 60

Two widely-used symbols:

To be played as quickly as possible

Prolonged note

Note-head systems:

Listed from longest to shortest

Systems of pauses and holds:

Listed from shortest to longest

Ritard and accelerando symbols:

Ritard

Accelerando

Symbols linked non-spatially to time:

System indicating the number of notes per second

8-12;   12-16;   16 or more;   20 or more

Number of notes per second

Number of seconds of silence

Excerpt from "A New Look for New Sounds" by MARJORY IRVIN from *Clavier* (April 1973). Used by Permission of *Clavier*, 1418 Lake Street, Evanston, Illinois 60204.

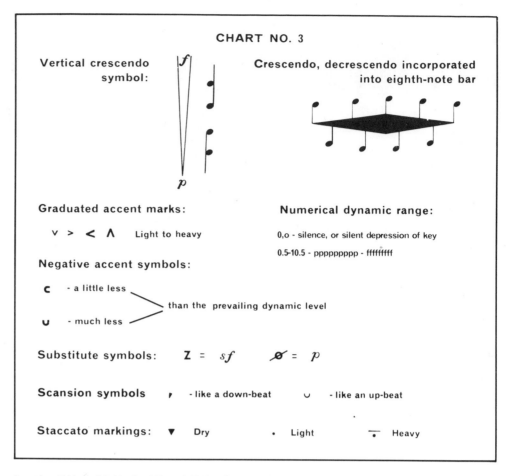

CHART NO. 3

Vertical crescendo symbol:

Crescendo, decrescendo incorporated into eighth-note bar

Graduated accent marks:

v > < Λ   Light to heavy

Negative accent symbols:

c - a little less

u - much less

than the prevailing dynamic level

Numerical dynamic range:

0,o - silence, or silent depression of key

0.5-10.5 - ppppppppp - fffffffff

Substitute symbols: Z = sf   ø = p

Scansion symbols   , - like a down-beat   ∪ - like an up-beat

Staccato markings: ▼ Dry   • Light   ‗ Heavy

Excerpt from "A New Look for New Sounds" by MARJORY IRVIN from *Clavier* (April 1973). Used by Permission of *Clavier*, 1418 Lake Street, Evanston, Illinois 60204.

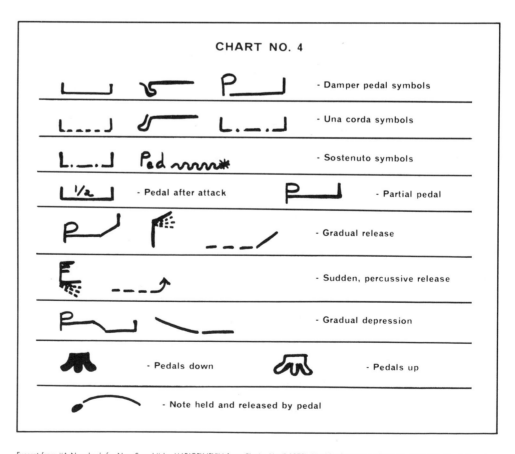

CHART NO. 4

- Damper pedal symbols

- Una corda symbols

- Sostenuto symbols

1/2 - Pedal after attack   - Partial pedal

- Gradual release

- Sudden, percussive release

- Gradual depression

- Pedals down   - Pedals up

- Note held and released by pedal

Excerpt from "A New Look for New Sounds" by MARJORY IRVIN from *Clavier* (April 1973). Used by Permission of *Clavier*, 1418 Lake Street, Evanston, Illinois 60204

CHART NO. 5

Improvisatory figures based on specific pitches

Free repretition of these notes; free rhythm

Notes within the compass to be played freely

Free repetition of these notes in any order, continuing for the length of the box

Repeat the group of notes for six seconds; very fast

Continue the pattern in any order

Free improvisatory figures:

Quasi-chromatic

Improvise

Slowly to top of keyboard

Graphic melodic outline

Trill or tremolo:

Beginning fast and gradually becoming slower

Excerpt from "A New Look for New Sounds" by MARJORY IRVIN from *Clavier* (April 1973). Used by Permission of *Clavier*, 1418 Lake Street, Evanston, Illinois 60204.

The reader should view the following pieces merely as samples of *some* of the new notational procedures found in contemporary music.

ELEMENTARY

°Adler, Samuel   *Gradus I,* #16
   Adventures in Time and Space, Vol. I, "As You Like It!" by Mary
      Mageau
   Covello, Stephen   *The Little Avant-Garde: A Piano Method for Pre-*
      Schoolers

**Examples of New
Notational Procedures**

INTERMEDIATE

°Adler, Samuel   *Gradus II,* #13
 Adler, Samuel   *Gradus II,* #19
°Finney, Ross Lee   *32 Piano Games,* I ("Middle, Bottom and Top")
°Finney, Ross Lee   *32 Piano Games,* XXII ("Black Notes and White Notes")
°Finney, Ross Lee   *32 Piano Games,* XXIX ("Windows")
°Mompou, Frederic   *Scènes d'Enfants,* "Cris dans la Rue" (all the pieces have new notation)

ADVANCED

°Cowell, Henry   *Piano Music,* "The Tides of Manaunaun"

Example 270
ADLER
Gradus I, #16
(m. 7-10)

Excerpt from #16 from *Gradus I* by SAMUEL ADLER. ' Copyright 1971 by Oxford University Press, Inc. Reprinted by Permission.

Example 271
ADLER
Gradus II, #13
(first three scores)

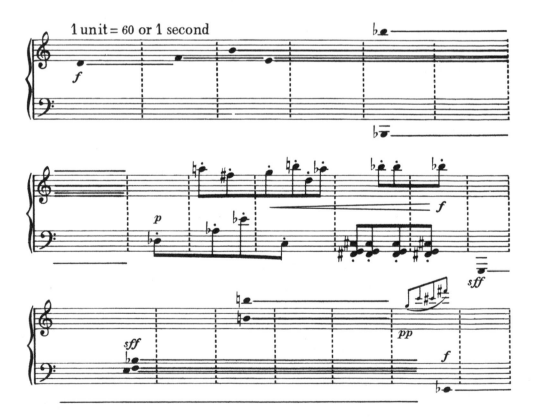

Excerpt from #13 from *Gradus II* by SAMUEL ADLER. ' Copyright 1971 by Oxford University Press, Inc. Reprinted by Permission.

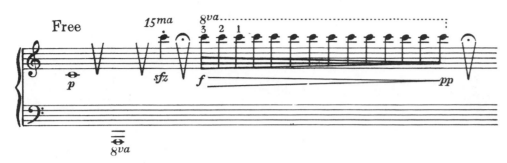

Example 272
FINNEY
32 Piano Games, I
(**"Middle, Bottom and Top"**)
(first score)

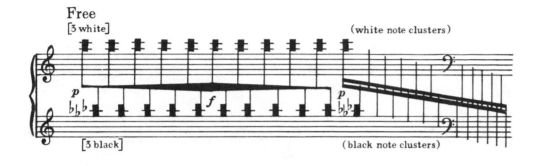

Example 273
FINNEY
32 Piano Games, XXII
(**"Black Notes and White Notes"**)
(first two scores)

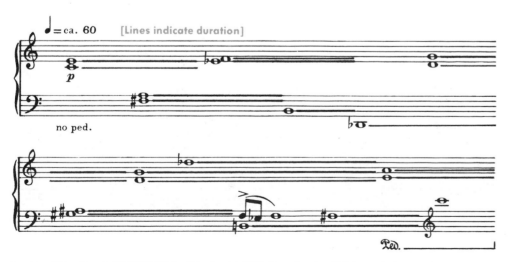

Example 274
FINNEY
32 Piano Games, XXIX
(**"Windows"**)
(first two scores)

Example 275
MOMPOU
Scènes d'Enfants
"Cris dans la Rue"
(m. 47-57)

Gai lointain

Excerpt from *Scènes d'Enfants* by FREDERIC MOMPOU.° Copyright 1921, Maurice Senart. Used by permission of the publisher, Editions Salabert.

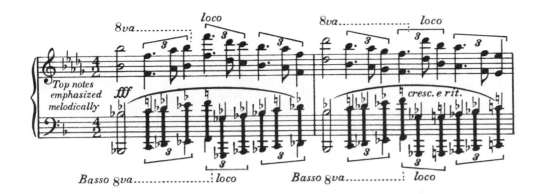

Example 276
COWELL
Piano Music
"The Tides of
Manaunaun"
(m. 22-25)

Excerpt from *Piano Music* by HENRY COWELL. Copyright by Associated Music Publishers, Inc. Used by Permission.

Aleatoric Music

Aleatoric or *chance* music is being written for all mediums including piano. This kind of writing allows the performer freedom to improvise or choose an arrangement of suggested patterns at given points in the piece. A time limit may or may not be imposed by the composer. An explanation of new notational symbols or performance procedure usually precedes an aleatoric piece.

Examples of Aleatoric Music

ELEMENTARY
Adventures in Time and Space, Vol. I, "Needles and Haystacks" by Lynn Freeman Olson
Covello, Stephen   *The Little Avant-Garde: A Piano Method for Pre-Schoolers*

INTERMEDIATE
°Adler, Samuel   *Gradus II*, #13 (see Example 271)
°Adler, Samuel   *Gradus II*, #16
°Adler, Samuel   *Gradus II*, #19
°Finney, Ross Lee   *32 Piano Games*, XXVIII ("Mountains")
°Finney, Ross Lee   *32 Piano Games*, XXX ("Mobile")
Horizons, Book 2, "White-Black" by J. Beckwith
Horizons, Book 2, "Wind-Harp" by J. Beckwith

ADVANCED
Horizons, Book 2, "If" by S. Dolin

[Patterns may be played in any order.]

Example 277
ADLER
Gradus II, **# 16**
(first five patterns)

Excerpt from ═16 from *Gradus II* by SAMUEL ADLER. ' Copyright 1971 by Oxford University Press, Inc. Reprinted by Permission.

Example 278
ADLER
Gradus II, **# 19**
(first score)

Excerpt from ═19 from *Gradus II* by SAMUEL ADLER. ' Copyright 1971 by Oxford University Press, Inc. Reprinted by Permission.

Example 279
FINNEY
32 Piano Games, XXVIII
("Mountains")
(fourth and fifth scores)

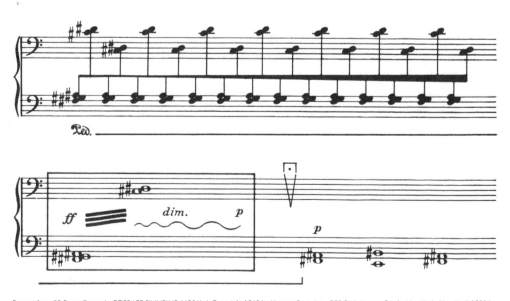

Excerpt from *32 Piano Games* by ROSS LEE FINNEY (P 66256). ' Copyright 1969 by Henmar Press, Inc., 373 Park Avenue South, New York, New York 10016. Reprint permission granted by the publisher.

Pioneered by Henry Cowell and Charles Ives, *clusters* are now common place to us in the late twentieth century whether played with the hand, arm or a board. Plucking strings inside the piano gives a harp effect and is used imaginatively by some composers. Some works even call for percussion mallets or marimba sticks to set the strings resonating.

INTERMEDIATE
°Adler, Samuel   *Gradus II*, #17

ADVANCED
°Cowell, Henry   *Piano Music*, "Aeolian Harp"
°Cowell, Henry   *Piano Music*, "The Banshee"
°Cowell, Henry   *Piano Music*, "Tiger"
°Hovhaness, Alan   *Fantasy Op. 16*

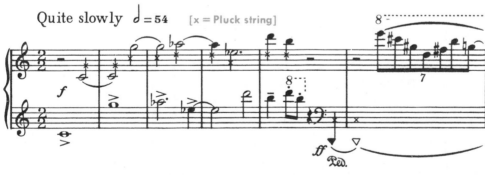

Example 280
FINNEY
32 Piano Games, XXX
("Mobile")
(first two scores)

Innovative Piano Effects

Examples of Innovative Effects

Example 281
ADLER
Gradus II, #17
(m. 1-11)

Example 282
COWELL
Piano Music
"Aeolian Harp"
(m. 1-8)

Tempo Rubato

Example 283
COWELL
Piano Music
"The Banshee"
(m. 1-11)

Tempo Rubato

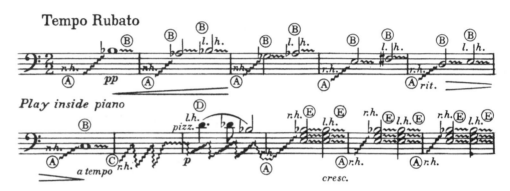

Example 284
COWELL
Piano Music
"Tiger"
(m. 4-7)

Tempo molto rubato, ad lib.

Example 285
HOVHANESS
Fantasy Op. 16
(page 5)

Inside piano, play
with marimba sticks

sempre con pedale

Tempo ad lib.

misterioso

Keyboard

Inside piano, play with soft plectrum

Excerpt from *Fantasy Op. 16* by ALAN HOVHANESS (P 6482). © Copyright 1969 by C. F. Peters Corporation, 373 Park Avenue South, New York, New York 10016. Reprint permission granted by the publisher.

1. Play and study a representative sampling of the piano pieces listed.

2. For additional resource reading, consult the following:

> Apel   *The Notation of Polyphonic Music, 900-1600*
> Cage   *Notations*
> Cope   *New Directions in Music*
> Dallin   *Techniques of Twentieth Century Composition*, Chapters 17 through 19.
> Irvin, Marjory   "A New Look for New Sounds," *Clavier*, April, 1973.
> Parrish   *The Notation of Medieval Music*
> Peyser   *The New Music*
> Pooler, Frank and Pierce, Brent   *New Choral Notation*
> Schwartz   *Electronic Music, A Listener's Guide*, Revised Edition (a layman's introduction to the field of electronic music)
> Strange   *Electronic Music—Systems, Techniques and Controls*

3. Read and play *Mosaics*, edited by Marguerite Miller, pages 14 through 19; pages 86 through 94. Compose a piece containing innovative piano effects and aleatoric elements.

4. Visit an electronic tape laboratory for a demonstration of the Moog synthesizer and other instruments.

5. Listen to an electronic piece; for example, *Antiphony IV, 1967* by Kenneth Gaburo (Nonesuch 71199, University of Illinois Contemporary Chamber Players).

6. Listen to these works of Edgard Varèse:

> *Deserts* (wind instruments, percussion and sounds produced electronically on tape)
> *Ionisation* (scored for percussion, friction and sibilation instruments) According to David Ewen, this contains "Varèse's greatest complexity of rhythmic and sonorous treatments." [11]

---

[11] Ewen, David   *The World of Twentieth Century Music*, p. 853.

Appendix A
Glossary of Terms

A

Active (tendency) tones in tonal music, the second, fourth, sixth and seventh degrees of the scale [see **Rest tones; Tendency tones**]

Added note chord a chord formed by adding tones to a tertian chord; the added second and sixth are most common

Aeolian mode the equivalent of the natural minor scale (A to A)

Aleatoric (chance) music music which gives the performer the freedom to improvise or choose an arrangement of suggested patterns

Alternating meters continuous alternation of two time signatures within a work [see **Changing meters**]

Arch form the organization of a piece into five or seven parts, resembling sonata-allegro form except the themes appear in reverse order in the recapitulation (A B C B A or A B C D C B A)

Asymmetric divisions unequal groupings within a conventional symmetric meter where the eighth note or sub-pulse remains constant; i.e., 4/4 grouped into 3+3+2/8

Asymmetric meters uneven grouping of beats, such as 5/4 (3+2 or 2+3) or 7/8 (3+2+2 or 4+3, etc.)

Asymmetric phrase a phrase of three, five or seven measures in length; i.e., not four or eight measures

Atonal cadence an ending or stopping point that may rest on any interval or chord

Atonality   the absence of a strong gravitational point and therefore, also, of tendency tones; all tones are given equal status [see **Free atonality; Serial atonality**]

Augmentation   the technique of increasing the rhythmic value of notes by a constant ratio; i.e., eighth notes become quarter notes [see **Diminution**]

B

Bichord   [see **Polychord**]

Bimodality   the use of two modes sounding simultaneously in separate layers [see **Polymodality**]

Bitonality   the use of two keys sounding simultaneously in separate layers [see **Polytonality**]

Blues   an improvisatory jazz style, consisting of a pattern of three four-measure phrases with the simple harmonic foundation of I, IV—I, and V—I. The melody contains "blues" notes, the flatted third and seventh tones of the scale.

C

Cadence   the ending of a phrase; temporary or final cessation of motion

Canon   a "follow-the-leader" type texture where each entering voice (or part) consists of the same melody as the initial voice. Canons are usually in two, three or four parts.

Chaconne   a form of Baroque music in which variations occur against a repeated harmonic progression [see **Passacaglia**]

Changing (fluctuating) meters   continuous changing of various time signatures within a work to notate irregular measure lengths [see **Alternating meters**]

Chant   [see **Plainsong**]

Chromatic scale   a twelve-tone scale by half steps with one note, the tonic, always functioning as the center of gravity; several spellings are possible [see **Dodecuple scale**]

Church (ecclesiastical) modes   ancient scales which bear the Grecian names of Ionian, Dorian, Phrygian, Lydian, Mixolydian, Aeolian and Locrian

Clusters   [see **Secundal chord**]

Complex chord   a chord formed by stacking as many as twelve different tones on top of each other (also known as skyscraper chord)

Cross-relation   a chromatically altered tone appearing in a different voice in the following chord; i.e., G in the alto on the first chord followed by a G♯ in the bass on the second chord

Cross-rhythms   unequal rhythms set against each other; i.e., two-eighths against three-eighths

D

Diatonic scales   the major and minor scales, without chromatic alteration

Diminution   the technique of decreasing the rhythmic value of notes by a constant ratio; i.e., half notes become quarter notes [see **Augmentation**]

Dissonant counterpoint   modern polyphony which allows any interval to be prominent; dissonant intervals need not resolve

Dodecuple (duodecuple) scale   a twelve-tone scale by half steps in which all tones have equal status; there is no gravitational point [see **Chromatic scale**]

Dorian mode   the equivalent of the natural minor scale with a raised sixth (D to D, using only white notes)

Expanded (free or extended) tonality   a tonality based on the dodecuple scale but which has a key center and ends on a tonic

Extended tonality   [see **Expanded tonality**]

Five-four ($\frac{5}{4}$) chord   a chord which contains both the intervals of a fourth and a fifth above the root; the interval of a third is not used [see **Non-tertian harmony**]

Fragmentation   pieces of sound punctuated by frequent rests; common in atonality

Free atonality   a type of atonality where all twelve tones of the dodecuple scale are used freely in any order; no tonic, as such, exists [see **Atonality; Serial Atonality**]

Free tonality   [see **Expanded tonality**]

Functional harmony   a traditional style where all chord progressions are generated by the hierarchy of the major-minor tonal system; all harmony in tonal music is functional [see **Non-functional harmony**]

Harmonics   a term given to the sound generated by depressing some keys silently while playing others; the sound produced is derived from the harmonic series of overtones (This definition applies only to piano music; harmonics are also possible on other instruments.)

Homophony   one prominent melody with harmonization [see **Monophony; Polyphony**]

Imitation   a contrapuntal device where a melodic idea is repeated immediately but in a different voice

Improvisation   the art of "making it up as you go along"; jazz improvisation involves melodic, rhythmic and tempo changes carried on over a harmonic skeleton by one soloist or by a group of players

Invention   a short contrapuntal form of two or three voices based upon a frequently recurring motive or phrase

Inversion   the technique of reversing the direction of each interval of a tone row or melody, creating a mirror image of the original; i.e., an ascending major third becomes a descending major third [see **Mirror writing**]

Inverted pedal point   a sustained or repeated tone occurring in an upper voice under which harmonies change [see **Pedal point**]

Invertible counterpoint   a contrapuntal device whereby two lines (or voices) are so constructed that they sound equally well regardless of vertical positioning; either one may be the upper or lower part. This is called inversion at the octave; however, other intervallic relationships are possible.

Ionian mode   the equivalent of the major scale (C to C)

Locrian mode   the equivalent of the natural minor scale with a lowered second and fifth (B to B, using only white notes)

Lydian mode   the equivalent of the major scale with a raised fourth (F to F, using only white notes)

M

Major-minor (split third) chord   a tertian chord which contains both a major and a minor third

Melodic doubling   the doubling of a melody at a uniform interval, such as a perfect fourth or a minor sixth

Mirror writing (reflection)   a contrapuntal device similar to inversion but occurring simultaneously instead of in linear sequence [see **Inversion**]

Mixolydian mode   the equivalent of the major scale with a lowered seventh (G to G, using only white notes)

Modal interchange   the mixing of several different major or minor-sounding modes in close succession

Modality (modalism)   the use of the ancient church modes

Modulation   in tonal music, the movement from one key to another

Monophony   a single melody [see **Homophony; Polyphony**]

N

Neo-classicism   a twentieth century revival of Baroque (and earlier) forms and textures, with particular emphasis on the contrapuntal style and dissonant linearity

Neo-modalism   a twentieth century usage of modal melodies harmonized with progressions from the major-minor system, including many seventh and ninth chords

Non-accented rhythms   [see **Prose rhythms**]

Non-chordal tone   a decorative tone foreign to the prevailing harmony which resolves eventually to a chord tone; i.e., passing tone, suspension, etc.

Non-functional harmony   a style where no heirarchy controls progressions; any relationship of chords is possible [see **Functional harmony**]

Non-tertian harmony   a system with chords built in intervals other than thirds [see **Five-four chord; Quartal chord; Quintal chord; Secundal chord; Tertian chord**]

O

Organum   an ancient texture consisting of parallel fourths (or fifths) and octaves

Ostinato   a recurring, short accompaniment pattern in the bass, usually with strong rhythmic implications

Out-of-phase   a repeated pattern that does not coincide with the meter

P

Pandiatonicism   a style of writing wherein the diatonic scale is employed without its traditional hierarchy of harmonic and melodic functions; a reaction against chromaticism, also called "white-note" writing

Passacaglia   a form of Baroque music in which variations occur over a repeated melodic pattern, usually in the bass [see **Chaconne**]

Pedal point   a sustained or repeated bass tone over which harmonies change [see **Inverted pedal point**]

Pentatonic scale   a five-tone scale of any intervallic pattern; most commonly represented by the arrangement of the black keys of the keyboard, any tone of which may be designated as a tonic

Phrygian mode   the equivalent of the natural minor scale with a lowered second (E to E, using only white notes)

Plainsong   an ancient style of free-flowing single line melody sometimes referred to as chant, plainchant or Gregorian chant

Pointillism   an atonal, fragmentary style in which continuous solid lines and textures are avoided

Polychord   a chordal structure formed by stacking two or more chords, keeping each one intact as a unit and spatially separated from the other. Two stacked chords are often referred to as a bichord.

Polymeter (polyrhythm)   the simultaneous use of more than one meter or rhythmic pattern; bar lines may or may not coincide

Polymodality   the use of two or more modes sounding simultaneously in separate layers [see **Bimodality**]

Polyphony   two or more independent melodies sounding simultaneously [see **Homophony; Monophony**]

Polytonality   the use of two or more keys sounding simultaneously in separate layers [see **Bitonality**]

Prose rhythms   free-flowing speech rhythms with little or no metric pulse

Pulsating rhythm   repeated notes with relentless, driving energy; sometimes an ostinato

Quartal chord   a chord built in intervals of fourths [see **Non-tertian harmony**]

Quintal chord   a chord built in intervals of fifths [see **Non-tertian harmony**]

Ragtime   a jazz adaptation for piano

Rest tones   in tonal music, the first, third and fifth degrees of the scale [see **Active tones**]

Retrograde   the technique of repeating the original tones of a tone row or melody backwards

Retrograde inversion   the technique of repeating the original tones of a tone row or melody backwards and upside-down [see **Retrograde; Inversion**]

Row   an assigned order given to tones; used in serial atonality

Secundal (cluster) chord   a chord built in intervals of seconds [see **Non-tertian harmony**]

Serial atonality   a type of atonality where tones are selected and pre-arranged into a set order or row which becomes the basis of both melodic and harmonic evolution [see **Atonality; Free Atonality**]

Serial chords   chords formed from the sectioning of a tone row into various size groups of tones and the arranging of them in vertical order

Shifted accents   irregular, unpredictable accents; usually occurring in changing meter contexts

Shifted tonality   a sudden shift to another key without the benefit of a gradual modulation

Syncopation   the displacement of an accent in an established meter from a strong beat to a weaker beat

Synthetic scale   any original, unconventional scale created by the composer

T

Tendency tones in tonal music, tones which need resolution; i.e., active tones, such as the seventh or leading tone; chordal dissonances, such as the seventh; chromatically altered tones [see **Active tones**]

Tertian chord a chord built in intervals of thirds [see **Non-tertian harmony**]

Texture density resulting from the combination of parts; i.e., thin, dense, linear

Tone clusters [see **Secundal chord**]

Tone row [see **Row**]

Tonic the first degree of the scale and gravitational point in tonal music; the name of the chord built on the first degree

Transposed modes modern usage of the church modes which allows them to begin on any degree of the scale; i.e., Dorian beginning on A and using an F♯

Transposition in serial writing, the appearance of a given row beginning on a new tone

Triad a three-note chord

Tritone an interval formed by three whole steps, outlining a diminished fifth or an augmented fourth

U

Unison writing the doubling of a melody at the octave, with the lines separated by two or more octaves (in different registers)

V

Variation the restatement of a pattern (usually melodic) with various changes in pitch and/or rhythm

W

Wholetone scale a six-tone or hexatonic scale consisting only of whole steps; only two such scales are possible, each starting on adjacent half steps; various spellings are possible

"Wrong-note" writing a technic of writing that disrupts simple melodies or harmonies with obvious "wrong" notes

Appendix B
The Tonal Period and Its Gradual Breakdown

The three-hundred-year period from 1600 to 1900, beginning with the predecessors of Bach (i.e., Frescobaldi, Buxtehude) and extending through the lifetimes of Wagner and Brahms, is sometimes called the "common practice" period because all works written during this time had one primary element in common, *tonality*. (The old church modes were still somewhat in use during 1600 but dwindled completely by the end of the century.) Tonal works may be described as being in a certain *key*, major or minor, which functions as the gravitational point of departure and return. The movement from one tonal center to another, called *modulation*, is a basic structural ingredient. For example, the *binary* form, typical of Baroque dance suites and Scarlatti sonatas, is monothematic and consists of two repeated sections—A :‖ B. :‖ . The first section modulates from the tonic to the dominant key, and the second continues in the dominant and eventually returns back to the tonic. (If the piece begins in minor, the modulation is usually to the relative major.) The *ternary* form consists of a contrasting middle section—new theme and different key—between a theme and its repetition (ABA). Authentic cadences, V - I, punctuate the sections and confirm the prevailing tonality. Half, plagal, deceptive and Phrygian cadences are also common in the period.

"Keyishness" is also responsible for the hierarchy that controls the progression and resolution of chords, referred to as *functional harmony*. Each chord is *tertian* (built in thirds) and bears the name of its relationship to the tonic, as follows:

Tonic   key center, point of final rest — CEG (key of C)
Supertonic   above the tonic — DFA

Mediant   midway between the tonic and dominant — EGB

Subdominant   the dominant below the tonic (five notes lower) — FAC

Dominant   fifth note of scale and next in importance to tonic — GBD

Submediant   midway between tonic and lower dominant (subdominant) — ACE

Leading Tone   one half-step below the tonic and leads to it — BDF

These diatonic chords are classified into two categories: *Primary* (I, IV, V) and *Secondary* (ii, iii, vi, vii°). Primary triads contain all the degrees of the scale (major or minor), so their principal role is to establish the tonality. Secondary triads provide contrast and color and may even substitute on occasion for primary triads.

Progression is largely determined by the resolution of tendency tones of which there are three types: *active degrees* of the scale which tend to resolve to rest tones (7-8, 2-1, 4-3, 6-5); *altered tones* which usually resolve stepwise in the direction of alteration; and *dissonant intervals* which "want" to resolve to consonant ones. This sets up for the listener the element of expectancy which, when achieved, brings satisfaction; when delayed or aborted, creates distress or tension.

Other features common to the tonal period are independence of melodic lines, retention of the same meter throughout, moderate range and relatively simple rhythmic textures.

The breakdown of this tonal "system" came about gradually, for each composer inherited a tradition and then built upon it. Bach exploited polyphony; Haydn and Mozart developed classical form; Beethoven emancipated form by allowing the human spirit to initiate musical expression; Chopin wove chromatic webs and Schumann explored the possibilities of syncopation. Then Wagner startled the musical world by carrying chromatic harmony to the ultimate in his operas, *Tristan und Isolde* and *Parsifal*. Evaded cadences and irregular resolutions of dissonant chords produced long, unbroken passages which meandered from key to key or dissolved all sense of key. Functional harmony gave way to non-functional, where harmonic color and emotive whim governed the choice of chords. Meanwhile, in France, the Belgian organist, Cesar Franck, was irregularly resolving augmented sixth chords, employing remote second and third relationships, modulating incessantly and tampering with the ancient modes. The combination of these and other innovations had a subtle but marked impact upon the status of tonality and the common practice of the past.

More overt were the explorations of Debussy in the use of sound-for-sound's-sake to portray shades of light and color, trying to produce in his music the effects his artist and poet friends were creating. In addition to non-functional harmony, where there is no hierarchy to force certain prescribed progressions and resolutions of chords, he recalled the archaic modes and organum (parallel fourths and fifths), employed the pentatonic, wholetone and exotic scales, balanced works over long pedal points and created flexible, fluid non-accentuated musical phrases reflective of the French language.

By the early twentieth century, two new and distinct paths were opening up: one toward the organization of the twelve tones to give chromatic music order and form, and the other toward less chromatic or "white-note" writing. Schoenberg and Stravinsky led these trends respectively. In addition, such composers as Hindemith and Bartok continued to exploit the free use of all twelve tones, resulting in an expanded tonality.

Appendix C
Bibliography

Theory

Apel, Willi. *The Notation of Polyphonic Music, 900-1600,* Fifth Edition. Cambridge, Mass.: Medieval Academy of America, 1961.

Cage, John. *Notations.* New York: The Something Else Press, 1969.

Carlson, Effie B. *A Bio-Bibliographical Dictionary of Twelve-Tone and Serial Composers.* Metuchen, N.J.: The Scarecrow Press, 1970. [uses twentieth century piano literature as framework of discussion]

Christ, William and Richard DeLone, Vernon Kliewer, Lewis Rowell, William Thompson. *Materials and Structure of Music, Vol. II,* Second Edition. Englewood Cliffs, N.J.: Prentice-Hall, Inc., 1973.

Cone, Edward T. *Musical Form and Musical Performance.* New York; W.W. Norton and Co., Inc., 1968.

Cooper, Grosvenor W. *The Rhythmic Structure of Music.* Chicago: University of Chicago Press, 1960. [technical]

Creston, Paul. *Principles of Rhythm.* New York: Franco Colombo Publications, 1964.

Dallin, Leon. *Techniques of Twentieth Century Composition,* Second Edition. Dubuque, Iowa: William C. Brown Co., Publishers, 1964.

Eschman, Karl H. *Changing Forms in Modern Music,* Second Edition. Boston: E.C. Schirmer Music Co., 1967.

Graves, William L. *Twentieth-Century Fugue.* Washington D.C.: Catholic University of America, 1962.

Theory (continued)

Hanson, Howard. *The Harmonic Materials of Modern Music: Resources of the Tempered Scale.* New York: Irvington Publishers, Inc., 1960.

Marquis, G. Welton. *Twentieth Century Music Idioms.* Englewood Cliffs, N.J.: Prentice-Hall, Inc., 1964. [contrapuntal approach; contains a helpful bibliography]

Messaien, Olivier. *The Technique of My Musical Language,* translated by John Satterfield. Paris: Alphonse Leduc et Cie., 1950.

Nallin, Walter E. *The Musical Idea: A Consideration of Music and Its Ways.* New York: The Macmillan Co., 1968

Parrish, Carl. *The Notation of Medieval Music.* New York: W.W. Norton and Co., Inc., 1959.

Perle, George. *Serial Composition and Atonality: An Introduction to the Music of Schoenberg, Berg and Webern,* Third Edition. Berkeley and Los Angeles: University of California Press, 1972.

Persichetti, Vincent. *Twentieth-Century Harmony.* New York: W.W. Norton and Co., Inc., 1961.

Pooler, Frank and Brent Pierce. *New Choral Notation.* New York: Walton Music Corp., 1971.

Reti, Rudolph. *Tonality in Modern Music.* New York: The Macmillan Co., 1962.

Schwartz, Elliott. *Electronic Music, A Listener's Guide,* Revised Edition. New York: Praeger Publishers, Inc., 1975.

Searle, Humphrey. *Twentieth-Century Counterpoint.* Clinton Corners, N.Y.: John de Graff, Inc., 1954.

Starer, Robert. *Rhythmic Training.* New York: MCA Music, 1969.

Strange, Allen. *Electronic Music: Systems, Techniques and Controls.* Dubuque, Iowa: William C. Brown Co., Publishers, 1972.

Ulehla, Ludmela. *Contemporary Harmony.* New York: The Free Press, a division of The Macmillan Co., 1966.

Vincent, John N. *The Diatonic Modes in Modern Music.* Hollywood: Curlew Music Publishers, Inc., 1974.

Wollner, Gertrude Price. *Improvisation in Music.* Boston: Bruce Humphries, Inc., 1963.

General

Austin, William W. *Music in the 20th Century.* New York: W.W. Norton and Co., Inc., 1966. [contains a 110-page bibliography with comments]

Chase, Gilbert. *America's Music: From the Pilgrims to the Present,* Revised Edition. New York: McGraw-Hill Book Co., Inc., 1966.

Cope, David H. *New Directions in Music—1950-1970.* Dubuque, Iowa: William C. Brown Co., Publishers, 1971.

Deri, Otto. *Exploring Twentieth-Century Music.* New York: Holt, Rinehart & Winston, Inc., 1968.

Ewen, David. *The World of Twentieth Century Music.* Englewood Cliffs, N.J.: Prentice-Hall, Inc., 1968.

Ghiselin, Brewster (ed.). *The Creative Process, A Symposium* (Roger Sessions). New York: A Mentor Book, The New American Library of World Literature, Inc., 1952.

Hansen, Peter S. *An Introduction to Twentieth Century Music*, Third Edition. Boston: Allyn and Bacon, Inc., 1971. [contains a list of composers by birth from 1860-1928]

Hindemith, Paul. *A Composer's World: Horizons and Limitations*. Gloucester, Mass.: Peter Smith Publisher, Inc., 1961. [lectures given at Harvard in 1949-1950]

Lang, Paul Henry (ed.). *Stravinsky: A New Appraisal of His Work*. New York: W.W. Norton and Co., Inc., 1963.

Leibowitz, Rene. *Schoenberg and His School*, translated by Dika Newlin. New York: Da Capo Press, Inc. 1970.

Machlis, Joseph. *Introduction to Contemporary Music*. New York: W.W. Norton and Co., Inc., 1961. [noteworthy are the Appendix I—basic concepts of melody, harmony, tonality, rhythm and meter, tempo, dynamics, instruments of the orchestra, form and overtone series; Appendix III—bibliography; and Appendix V—a chronological list of modern composers, world events and principal figures in literature and the arts]

Oxford Book of Carols, edited by Percy Dearmer, R. Vaughn Williams and Martin Shaw. New York: Oxford University Press, Inc., 1964.

Peyser, Joan. *The New Music: The Sense Behind the Sound*. New York: Dell Publishing Co., Inc., 1972.

Salzman, Eric. *Twentieth-Century Music: An Introduction*, Second Edition. Englewood Cliffs, N.J.: History of Music Series, Prentice-Hall, Inc., 1974.

Schoenberg, Arnold. *Style and Idea: Selected Writings of Arnold Schoenberg*. New York: St. Martin's Press, 1975.

Sessions, Roger. *The Musical Experience of Composer, Performer, Listener*. Princeton: Princeton University Press, 1971.

Stevens, Halsey. *The Life and Music of Bela Bartok*, Revised Edition. New York: Oxford University Press, Inc., 1964.

Stravinsky, Igor. *An Autobiography*. New York: The Norton Library, W.W. Norton and Co., Inc., 1962.

Ward, William. *Examples for the Study of Musical Style*, Third Edition. Dubuque, Iowa: William C. Brown Co., Publishers, 1970.

Wennerstrom, Mary. *Anthology of Twentieth Century Music*. New York: Appleton-Century-Crofts, Educational Division, Meredith Corp., 1969.

Adler, Samuel. "Problems of Teaching Composition in Our Colleges Today," *American Music Teacher*, (November-December 1963).

Bullard, Ethel. "Preparing Our Students for College Entrance," *Illinois State Music Teachers Association Newsletter*, (February 1967).

Burge, David. "An Approach to the Performance of Twentieth-Century Music." *Clavier*, (March-April 1963).

Carlsen, James. "Music Theory—Preparation for College Entrance," *American Music Teacher*, (April-May 1969).

Carpenter, Hoyle and others, compilers. "A Suggested List of Readings in Music History and Theory for the Studio Teacher." *American Music Teacher*, (July-August 1963).

Cazedessus, Duchein. "Contemporary Sounds in Piano Teaching Literature," *Handbook for Piano Teachers*. Evanston, Ill.: Summy-Birchard Co., 1958.

Articles (continued)

Eagle, Nance. "Ear-Training for the Pre-College Student," *American Music Teacher*, (February-March 1970).

Ehle, Robert C. "The Two Major Stylistic Episodes of 20th Century Music," *American Music Teacher*, (June-July 1975).

Ganz, Rudolph. "Evaluating New Music," *Clavier*, (October 1965 through January 1967; September 1968). [This music is for the more advanced pianist.]

Ganz, Rudolph. "Seeking Tomorrow's Beauty," *Clavier*, (November-December 1965).

Grentzer, Rose Marie. "Preparation of the Music Educator to Use the Music of His Own Time." *Inter-American Bulletin*, (November 1966).

Hitchcock, Wiley H. "Frontiers in Music Today," *American Music Teacher*, (July-August 1961).

Hunkins, Arthur. "A Teacher Views Problems of the Student Composer," *American Music Teacher*, (February-March 1968).

Irvin, Marjory. "A New Look for New Sounds," *Clavier*, (April 1973).

Kushner, David. "Ernest Bloch: Teacher-Thinker," *American Music Teacher*, (September-October 1968).

McAllister, David. "Teaching the Music Teacher to Use the Music of His Own Culture," *Inter-American Music Bulletin*, (November 1966).

Montandon, Blaise. "What Makes Modern Music Modern?," *American Music Teacher*, (January-February 1959).

O'Connor, Justine. "Theory: Its Role in the Learning Process," *American Music Teacher*, (February-March 1967).

Sabrack, Harold. "Traditional vs. Experimental Trends in 20th Century Music," *American Music Teacher*, (April-May 1970).

Slenczynska, Ruth. "Preparing Piano Students for College Entrance," *Clavier*, (February 1967).

Smith, Catherine A. "Piano Music of the Twentieth Century," *Illinois State Music Teachers Association Newsletter*, (October 1966).

Stein, Leon. "Approaches to the Pedagogy of Form and Analysis," *American Music Teacher*, (July-August 1964).

Stone, Marion Brown. "Reading Rhythm," *Clavier*, (November 1971).

Walton, Charles W., "Analyzing Analysis," *Music Educators Journal*, (February 1969).

Yuhasz, Sister Marie Joy, O.P., "Black Composers...and Their Piano Music," Part I, *American Music Teacher*, (February-March 1970); Part II, *American Music Teacher*, (April-May 1970).

Lists of Music and Books

Butler, Stanley. *Guide to the Best in Contemporary Piano Music: An Annotated List of Graded Solo Piano Music, Published since 1950, Vols. I and II.* Metuchen, N.J.: The Scarecrow Press, 1973.

Friskin, James and Irwin Freundlich. *Music for the Piano: A Handbook of Concert and Teaching Material from 1580 to 1952*, Revised Edition. New York: Dover Publications, Inc., 1973.

Hinson, Maurice. *Guide to the Pianist's Repertoire.* Bloomington, Ind.: Indiana University Press, 1973.

Kern, Alice and Helen Titus. *The Teacher's Guidebook to Piano Literature*, revised by Alice Kern. Ann Arbor, Mich.: Edward Brothers, Inc., 1964.

Kirby, F.E. *Short History of Keyboard Music*. New York: The Free Press, a division of The Macmillan Co., 1966. [long chapter on twentieth century music]

Newman, William S. *A Selected List of Music Recommended for Piano Students*, Revised Edition. Chapel Hill, N.C.: University of North Carolina, Bureau of Adult Residential Education, Extension Division, 1965.

Rezits, Joseph and Gerald Deatsman. *The Pianist's Resource Guide: Piano Music in Print and Literature on the Pianistic Art*. Park Ridge, Ill.: Pallma Music Corp., 1974.

(List of new publications also appear in such magazines as *Clavier, Piano Quarterly, American Music Teacher*, etc.)

Austin, William W. *Music in the 20th Century*. New York: W.W. Norton and Co., Inc., 1966 [chapters 11 and 15; bibliography]

Blesh, Rudi. *Shining Trumpets: A History of Jazz,* Second Edition. New York: Da Capo Press, Inc., 1975.

Blesh, Rudi and Harriet Janis. *They All Played Ragtime,* Revised Edition. New York: Quick Fox, Inc., 1966-1971.

Hansen, Peter S., *An Introduction to Twentieth Century Music,* Third Edition. Boston: Allyn and Bacon, Inc., 1971. [Part I, chapter 5]

Mehegan, John. *Contemporary Styles for the Jazz Pianist*. New York: Sam Fox Publishing Co., Inc., 1965.

Mehegan, John. *Jazz Improvisation, Books 1-4*. New York: Sam Fox Publishing Co., Inc., 1965.

Mehegan, John. *The Jazz Pianist*. New York: Sam Fox Publishing Co., Inc., 1965.

Mehegan, John. *Studies in Jazz Harmony*. New York: Sam Fox Publishing Co., Inc., 1965.

Mehegan, John. *Styles for the Jazz Pianist*. New York: Sam Fox Publishing Co., Inc., 1965.

Mehegan, John. *Touch and Rhythm Techniques for the Jazz Pianist*. New York: Sam Fox Publishing Co., Inc., 1965.

Morgan and Horricks. *Modern Jazz, A Survey of Developments since 1939*. London: 1957.

Sargeant, Winthrop. *Jazz, Hot and Hybrid,* Third Edition. New York: Da Capo Press, Inc., 1975.

Stearns, Marshall. *The Story of Jazz*. New York: Oxford University Press, Inc., 1970.

Ulanov, Barry. *A Handbook of Jazz*. Westport, Conn.: Greenwood Press, Inc., 1975.

Ulanov, Barry. *A History of Jazz in America*. New York: Da Capo Press, Inc., 1972.

Jazz — Books

Jazz — Articles

Davis, Edward. "Jazz, Percussion, and Piano Classes," *Clavier*, (May-June 1969).

Ehle, Robert. "Jazz Classics or Classical Jazz (The Story of Third Stream Jazz)," *American Music Teacher*, (September-October 1972).

Konowitz, Bert. "Beginning Jazz," *Clavier*, (December 1967).

Konowitz, Bert. "Jazz Chords," *Clavier*, (October 1968).

Lowder, Jerry. "Jazzing Up the Theory Class," *Clavier*, (December 1968).

Mehegan, John. "How-to-do-it" Series on Jazz, *Clavier*, (October 1965 through December 1966).

Nevin, Mark. "What is Jazz," *Clavier*, (September 1965).

Appendix D
List of Examples

Alphabetical

Numerical

Reference List of Selected Contemporary Piano Music

Adler, Samuel   *Gradus I* (20 Studies). Oxford University Press, Inc.°   **ELEMENTARY**
Adventures in Times and Space, Vol. I (Studies for Contemporary Music).
    Schmitt, Hall and McCreary Co.
Bartok, Bela   *First Term at the Piano*. Boosey & Hawkes, Inc.; Edwin F.
    Kalmus.†
Bartok, Bela   *For Children, Vol. I* Alfred Music Co., Inc.; Boosey & Hawkes,
    Inc.; General Words and Music Co.; International Music Co.;
    Edwin F. Kalmus.
Bartok, Bela   *Mikrokosmos, Vol. I.* Boosey & Hawkes, Inc.
Bartok, Bela   *Mikrokosmos, Vol. II.* Boosey & Hawkes, Inc.
Bartok, Bela   *Ten Easy Pieces*. Alfred Music Co. Inc.; Boosey & Hawkes, Inc.;
    Edwin F. Kalmus; MCA Music. [some are Intermediate]
Bela Bartok: An Introduction to the Composer and his Music, edited by Joseph
    Banowetz. General Words and Music Co. [some are Intermediate]

°For complete information, see **Publishers' Addresses**.

†When an edition is available from more than one source, the author has
  suggested several publishers. This listing is not intended to be exclusive; the
  pieces may be found in additional sources such as collections or anthologies.

Bittner, Francis   *The Creatures Speak* (Easy Keyboard Explorations). Carl Fischer, Inc.

Contemporary Collection, Revised Edition, selected and edited by Goldstein, Kern, Larimer, Ross and Weiss. Summy-Birchard Co. [some are Intermediate]

Contemporary Piano Literature, Book 1   (Frances Clark Library). Summy-Birchard Co.

Contemporary Piano Literature, Book 2   (Frances Clark Library). Summy-Birchard Co.

Contempo 1, selected and edited by Mary Elizabeth Clark. Myklas Press.

Contempo 2, selected and edited by Mary Elizabeth Clark. Myklas Press.

Contempos in Crimson, selected and edited by Mary Elizabeth Clark. Myklas Press.

Contempos in Jade, selected and edited by Mary Elizabeth Clark. Myklas Press.

Contempos in Orchid, selected and edited by Mary Elizabeth Clark. Myklas Press.

Contempos in Sapphire, selected and edited by Mary Elizabeth Clark. Myklas Press.

Covello, Stephen   *The Little Avante-Garde: A Piano Method for Pre-Schoolers*. Schroeder & Gunther.

Dello Joio, Norman   *Suite for the Young*. Edwards B. Marks Music Corp.

Diamond, David   *Album for the Young*. Elkan-Vogel, Inc.

Finney, Ross Lee   *32 Piano Games*. Henmar Press, Inc. [many are Intermediate]

Frackenpohl, Arthur   *Circus Parade*. Oxford University Press, Inc.

Frost, Bernice   *In a Space Ship*. J. Fischer and Bros.

Grove, Roger   *Jazz About*. General Words and Music Co. [some are Intermediate]

Kabalevsky, Dmitri   *Five Sets of Variations Op. 51*. MCA Music.

Kavalevsky, Dmitri   *24 Little Pieces for Children Op. 39*. Alfred Music Co. Inc.; International Music Co., Edwin F. Kalmus; Edward B. Marks Music Corp.; MCA Music; G. Schirmer, Inc.

Kraehenbuehl, David   *Calendar Scenes*. Schmitt, Hall and McCreary Co.

Kraehenbuehl, David   *Jazz and Blues, Book 1* (Frances Clark Library). Summy-Birchard Co.

Kraehenbuehl, David   *Jazz and Blues, Book 2* (Frances Clark Library). Summy-Birchard Co.

Kraehenbuehl, David   *Jazz and Blues, Book 3* (Frances Clark Library). Summy-Birchard Co.

Mack, Glenn   *Adventures in Modes and Keys* (50 Short Piano Studies). Summy-Birchard Co.

Masters of Our Day, edited by Saminsky and Freed. Carl Fischer, Inc. [many are Intermediate]

Noona, Walter and Noona, Carol   *The Contemporary Performer, Book 2* (Mainstreams Piano Method). Heritage Music Press.

Olson, Lynn Freeman   *Menagerie*. Oxford University Press, Inc.

Persichetti, Vincent   *Parades for Piano Op. 57*. Elkan-Vogel, Inc.

Piano Literature, Vol. II, edited by Jane Smisor Bastien. General Words and Music Co.

Rollino, Joseph and Sheftel, Paul   *Festivities* (Four-Hand Duets). Carl Fischer, Inc.

Shostakovitch, Dmitri   *Six Children's Pieces*. Edwin F. Kalmus; MCA Music, C. F. Peters Corp.

Siegmeister, Elie   *American Kaleidoscope*. Sam Fox Publishing, Inc. [many are Intermediate]

Stevens, Everett   *Six Modal Miniatures*. Oliver Ditson Co.

Stravinsky, Igor   *Les Cinq Doigts (The Five Fingers)*. J & W Chester, Ltd.

Stravinsky, Soulima   *Piano Music for Children (Klaviermusik für Kinder), Vol. I*. C. F. Peters Corp.

Stravinsky, Soulima   *Piano Music for Children (Klaviermusik für Kinder), Vol. II*. C. F. Peters Corp.

Adler, Samuel *Gradus II* (20 Studies). Oxford University Press, Inc.

Adventures in Time and Space, Vol. II (Studies for Contemporary Music). Schmitt, Hall and McCreary Co.

Adventures in Time and Space, Vol. III (Studies for Contemporary Music). Schmitt, Hall and McCreary Co.

Adventures in Time and Space, Vol. IV (Studies for Contemporary Music). Schmitt, Hall and McCreary Co.

Adventures in Time and Space, Vol. V (Studies for Contemporary Music). Schmitt, Hall and McCreary Co.

American Composers of Today (23 Piano Pieces). Edward B. Marks Music Corp.

American Music by Distinguished Composers, Book 2, edited by Isadore Freed. Theodore Presser Co.

Bartok, Bela *For Children, Vol. I.* Alfred Music Co. Inc.; Boosey & Hawkes, Inc.; General Words and Music Co.; International Music Co.; Edwin F. Kalmus.

Bartok, Bela *For Children, Vol. II.* Boosey & Hawkes, Inc.; Edwin F. Kalmus.

Bartok, Bela *Fourteen Bagatelles Op. 6.* Boosey & Hawkes, Inc.; Edwin F. Kalmus. [some are Advanced]

Bartok, Bela *Mikrokosmos, Vol. III.* Boosey & Hawkes, Inc.

Bartok, Bela *Mikrokosmos, Vol. IV.* Boosey & Hawkes, Inc.

Bartok, Bela *Mikrokosmos, Vol. V.* Boosey & Hawkes, Inc.

Bartok, Bela *Roumanian Folk Dances.* Boosey & Hawkes, Inc.

Bartok, Bela *Sonatina.* Boosey & Hawkes, Inc.; International Music Co.; Edwin F. Kalmus.

Bartok, Bela *Ten Easy Pieces.* Alfred Music Co. Inc.; Boosey & Hawkes, Inc.; Edwin F. Kalmus; MCA Music. [some are Elementary]

Bartok, Bela *Three Hungarian Folk-Tunes.* Boosey & Hawkes, Inc.; Edwin F. Kalmus.

Bela Bartok: An Introduction to the Composer and his Music, edited by Joseph Banowetz. General Words and Music Co. [some are Elementary]

Bloch, Ernest *Enfantines.* (10 Pieces for Children). Carl Fischer, Inc.

Casella, Alfredo *11 Children's Pieces.* Universal Edition A.G.

Contemporary Collection, Revised Edition, selected and edited by Goldstein, Kern, Larimer, Ross and Weiss. Summy-Birchard Co. [some are Elementary]

Contemporary Piano Literature, Book 3 (Frances Clark Library). Summy-Birchard Co.

Contemporary Piano Literature, Book 4 (Frances Clark Library). Summy-Birchard Co.

Contemporary Piano Literature, Book 5-6 (Frances Clark Library). Summy-Birchard Co.

Contemporary Piano Repertoire, Level 5, edited by Maurice Hinson and David Glover (David Carr Glover Piano Library). Belwin-Mills Publishing Corp.

Contemporary Piano Repertoire, Level 6, edited by Maurice Hinson and David Glover (David Carr Glover Piano Library). Belwin-Mills Publishing Corp.

Creston, Paul *Five Little Dances.* G. Schirmer, Inc.

Dello Joio, Norman *Lyric Pieces for the Young.* Edward B. Marks Music Corp.

Diamond, David *Alone at the Piano, Book 2.* Southern Music Publishing Co.

Fennimore, Joseph *Bits and Pieces.* Edward B. Marks Music Corp.

Fiala, George *Ten Postludes.* Waterloo Music Company, Ltd.

Fichandler, William *Ten Polytonal Compositions.* Belwin-Mills Publishing Corp.

Finney, Ross Lee *24 Piano Inventions.* Henmar Press, Inc.

Finney, Ross Lee *32 Piano Games.* Henmar Press, Inc. [some are Elementary]

Fletcher, Stanley *Street Scenes.* Summy-Birchard Co.

Fuleihan, Anis *Ionian Pentagon.* Boosey & Hawkes, Inc.

Ginastera, Alberto *12 American Preludes, Vol. I.* Carl Fischer, Inc. [some are Advanced; #2 is Difficult]

Goossens, Eugene *Kaleidoscope Op. 18.* J & W Chester, Ltd.

INTERMEDIATE (continued)

Grove, Roger   *Jazz About.* General Words and Music Co. [some are Elementary]

Harris, Roy   *Little Suite.* G. Schirmer, Inc.

Hindemith, Paul   *Easy Five-Tone Pieces (Kleine Klaviermusik).* Schott and Co.

Hopkins, Antony   *Sonatine for Piano.* Oxford University Press, Inc.

Horizons, Book 1. Waterloo Music Company, Ltd.

Horizons, Book 2. Waterloo Music Company, Ltd. [some are Advanced]

Hovhaness, Alan   *Mystic Flute Op. 22.* C. F. Peters Corp.

In the Mode, selected and edited by Mary Elizabeth Clark. Myklas Press.

Kabalevsky, Dmitri   *Children's Pieces Op. 27.* International Music Co.; Edwin F. Kalmus; MCA Music; C. F. Peters Corp.

Kabalevsky, Dmitri   *Easy Variations Op. 40 No. 1.* Edwin F. Kalmus.

Kabalevsky, Dmitri   *6 Preludes and Fugues Op. 61.* MCA Music.

Kabalevsky, Dmitri   *Sonatina Op. 13 No. 1.* Ashley Dealer's Service; International Music Co.; Edwin F. Kalmus; MCA Music; C. F. Peters Corp.; G. Schirmer, Inc.

Khachaturian, Aram   *Adventures of Ivan.* MCA Music; G. Schirmer, Inc.

Kraehenbuehl, David   *Jazz and Blues, Book 4* (Frances Clark Library). Summy-Birchard Co.

Kraehenbuehl, David   *Jazz and Blues, Book 5* (Frances Clark Library). Summy-Birchard Co.

Kraehenbuehl, David   *Jazz and Blues, Book 6* (Frances Clark Library). Summy-Birchard Co.

Krenek, Ernst   *12 Short Piano Pieces Op. 83.* G. Schirmer, Inc.

Kubik, Gail   *Sonatina for Piano.* Mercury Music, Inc.

Lloyd, Norman   *Episodes for Piano.* Elkan-Vogel, Inc. [many are Advanced]

Masters of Our Day, edited by Saminsky and Freed. Carl Fischer, Inc. [some are Elementary]

Mompou, Frederic   *Scenes d'Enfants.* Editions Salabert. [some are Advanced]

Mosaics (32 piano Pieces for Learning Musicianship), edited by Marguerite (Mainstreams Piano Method). Heritage Music Press.

Pentland, Barbara   *Echoes.* Waterloo Music Company, Ltd.

Pentland, Barbara   *Hands Across the C.* Waterloo Music Company, Ltd.

Pentland, Barbara   *Space Studies.* Waterloo Music Company, Ltd.

Persichetti, Vincent   *Little Piano Book.* Elkan-Vogel, Inc.

Persichetti, Vincent   *Piano Sonatinas Nos. 1-6.* Elkan-Vogel, Inc.

Piano Literature, Vol. III, edited by James Bastien. General Words and Music Co.

Pinto, Octavio   *Scenas Infantis (Memories of Childhood).* G. Schirmer, Inc.

Prokofiev, Serge   *Children's Pieces Op. 65.* Alfred Music Co. Inc.; Boosey & Hawkes; International Music Co.; Edwin F. Kalmus; MCA Music; G. Schirmer, Inc.

Prokofiev, Serge   *Four Pieces Op. 32.* International Music Co.; Edwin F. Kalmus.

Rea, John   *What You Will* (6 Polytonal Duets). A Jaymar Publication, Iroquois Press.

Rebikov, Vladimir   *Les Demon s'amusent.* G. Schirmer, Inc.

Rebikov, Vladimir   *Silhouettes Op. 31.* Associated Music Publishers, Inc.; G. Schirmer, Inc.

Schoenberg, Arnold   *6 Kleine Klavierstucke (6 Little Piano Pieces) Op. 19.* Belmont Music Publishers.

Schuman, William   *Three Piano Moods.* Merion Music, Inc.

Schuman, William   *Three-Score Set.* G. Schirmer, Inc.

Scott, Cyril   *Pastoral Suite.* Galaxy Music Corp.

Scott, Cyril   *Selected Works.* G. Schirmer, Inc. [some are Advanced]

Shostakovitch, Dmitri   *Dances of the Dolls.* Edwin F. Kalmus; MCA Music; C. F. Peters Corp.

Shostakovitch, Dmitri   *Three Fantastic Dances.* International Music Co.; Edwin F. Kalmus; Edward B. Marks Music Corp.; MCA Music.

Siegmeister, Elie   *American Kaleidoscope.* Sam Fox Publishing Company, Inc. [some are Elementary]

Starer, Robert   *Seven Vignettes for Piano.* MCA Music.
Starer, Robert   *Sketches in Color.* MCA Music.
Stravinsky, Soulima   *Six Sonatinas for Young Pianists.* C. F. Peters Corp.
Stravinsky, Soulima   *Three Inventions.* C. F. Peters Corp.
Studies in 20th Century Idioms, "Black and White" by Eldon Rathburn.
   Waterloo Music Company, Ltd.
Studies in 20th Century Idioms, "Intervals, Patterns, Shapes" by Brian
   Cherney. Waterloo Music Company, Ltd.
Studies in 20th Century Idioms, "Ostinette" by F.R.C. Clarke. Waterloo
   Music Company, Ltd.
Studies in 20th Century Idioms, "Six Little Etudes" by Gerhard Wuensch.
   Waterloo Music Company, Ltd.
Studies in 20th Century Idioms, "Variations on a Folk Song" by Keith Bissell.
   Waterloo Music Company, Ltd.
Tansman, Alexandre   *Pour les Enfants, 4th Set.* Associated Music Publishers.
Tcherepnin, Alexander   *Bagatelles Op. 5.* Heugel et Cie.; International
   Music Co.; MCA Music; G. Schirmer, Inc. [many are Advanced]
Toch, Ernst   *Echoes from a Small Town Op. 49* (Kleinstadtbilder). Schott
   and Co.
Toch, Ernst   *Reflections Op. 86.* Belwin-Mills Publishing Corp.
Toch, Ernst   *Three Little Dances Op. 85.* Belwin-Mills Publishing Corp.
The Twentieth Century, An Anthology of Piano Music, Vol. IV, edited by
   Denes Agay. Yorktown Music Press [many are Advanced]
The World of Modern Piano Music, edited by Denes Agay. MCA Music.

Barber, Samuel   *Excursions Op. 20.* G. Schirmer, Inc.
Bartok, Bela   *Allegro Barbaro.* Boosey & Hawkes, Inc.; Universal Edition.
Bartok, Bela   *Fourteen Bagatelles Op. 6.* Boosey & Hawkes; Edwin F.
   Kalmus. [some are Intermediate]
Bartok, Bela   *Improvisations Op. 20.* Boosey & Hawkes, Inc.
Bartok, Bela   *Mikrokosmos, Vol. VI.* Boosey & Hawkes, Inc.
Bartok, Bela   *Suite Op. 14.* Boosey & Hawkes; Universal Edition.
Bartok, Bela   *Three Rondos.* Boosey & Hawkes, Inc.
Bartok, Bela   *Two Roumanian Dances Op. 8a.* Boosey & Hawkes, Inc.;
   Edwin F. Kalmus.
Bernstein, Leonard   *Four Anniversaries (1948).* G. Schirmer, Inc.
Bolcom, William   *Graceful Ghost Rag.* Edward B. Marks Music Corp.
Bolcom, William   *Three Popular Rags.* Edward B. Marks Music Corp.
Britten, Benjamin   *Night-Piece (Notturno).* Boosey & Hawkes, Inc.
Chavez, Carlos   *Sonatina 1924.* Boosey & Hawkes, Inc.
Chavez, Carlos   *Ten Preludes 1937.* G. Schirmer, Inc.
Classic Piano Rags (Complete Original Music for 81 Rags), selected by Rudi
   Blesh. Dover Publications, Inc.
Copland, Aaron   *The Cat and the Mouse.* Boosey & Hawkes, Inc.
Cowell, Henry   *Piano Music.* Associated Music Publishers.
Creston, Paul   *Six Preludes Op. 38.* MCA Music.
Davis, Allan   *Razorback Reel.* Oxford University Press, Inc.
Debussy, Claude   *Preludes, Book 1.* Durand et Cie.
Debussy, Claude   *Preludes, Book 2.* Durand et Cie.
Dello Joio, Norman   *Piano Sonata No. 3.* Carl Fischer, Inc.
Dello Joio, Norman   *Prelude: To a Young Musician.* G. Schirmer, Inc.
Dello Joio, Norman   *Suite for Piano.* G. Schirmer, Inc.
51 Piano Pieces from the Modern Repertoire. G. Schirmer, Inc.
Francaix, Jean   *Scherzo.* Schott and Co.
Fuleihan, Anis   *Fugue.* Carl Fischer, Inc.
Fuleihan, Anis   *Sonatina No. 2.* MCA Music.
Gershwin, George   *Preludes for Piano.* Warner Bros. Publications, Inc.
Ginastera, Alberto   *12 American Preludes, Vol. I.* Carl Fischer, Inc. [some are
   Intermediate; #2 is Difficult]

**ADVANCED
(continued)**

Griffes, Charles   *Three Tone-Pictures Op. 5.* G. Schirmer, Inc.

Harris, Roy   *Piano Suite.* Belwin-Mills Publishing Corp.

Harris, Roy   *Toccata.* Carl Fischer, Inc.

Hindemith, Paul   *Ludus Tonalis.* Associated Music Publishers; Schott and Co.

Hindemith, Paul   *Sonata No. 2.* Schott and Co.

Hindemith, Paul   *Suite for Piano "1922" Op. 26.* Schott and Co.

Horizons, Book 2. Waterloo Music Company, Ltd. [many are Intermediate]

Hovhaness, Alan   *Fantasy Op. 16.* C. F. Peters Corp.

Ireland, John   *Sonatina.* Oxford University Press, Inc.

Joplin, Scott   *Collected Piano Works* (Rags, Waltzes, Marches). The New York Public Library and Belwin-Mills Publishing Corp. [many editions are published separately and in easier arrangements]

Kabalevsky, Dmitri   *24 Preludes Op. 38.* International Music Co.; Edwin F. Kalmus; Edward B. Marks Music Corp.; MCA Music; C. F. Peters Corp.

Kennan, Kent   *Three Preludes.* G. Schirmer, Inc.

Khachaturian, Aram   *Toccata.* Ashley Dealer's Service; International Music Co.; Edwin F. Kalmus; MCA Music; C. F. Peters Corp.; G. Schirmer, Inc.

Lees, Benjamin   *Toccata.* Alec Templeton, Inc.

Lloyd Norman   *Episodes for Piano.* Elkan-Vogel, Inc. [some are Intermediate]

Mehegan, John   *Jazz Preludes.* Sam Fox Publishing Co., Inc.

Milano, Robert   *Toccata.* Beekman Music, Inc.

Milhaud, Darius   *Saudades do Brazil, Book 1.* Associated Music Publishers; Schott and Co.

Milhaud, Darius   *Saudades do Brazil, Book 2.* Associated Music Publishers; Schott and Co.

Mompou, Frederic   *Scenes d'Enfants.* Editions Salabert. [some are Intermediate]

New Music for the Piano (Compilation of 22 Contemporary Composers), selected for Joseph Prostakoff. Lawson-Gould Music Publishers. [many are Difficult]

Peeters, Flor   *Toccata Op. 51a.* C. F. Peters Corp.

Piston, Walter   *Passacaglia.* Mercury Music, Inc.

Poulenc, Francis   *Mouvements Perpetuels.* J & W Chester, Ltd.

Poulenc, Francis   *Trois Pieces.* Mercury Music, Inc.

Prokofiev, Serge   *Four Pieces Op. 4.* Edwin F. Kalmus; MCA Music. ["Despair" is Difficult]

Prokofiev, Serge   *Sarcasms Op. 17.* Edwin F. Kalmus; MCA Music.

Prokofiev, Serge   *Visions Fugitives Op. 22.* Boosey & Hawkes, Inc.; International Music Co.; Edward B. Marks Music Corp.; MCA Music.

Rawsthorne, Alan   *Bagatelles.* Oxford University Press, Inc.

Riegger, Wallingford   *New and Old.* Boosey & Hawkes, Inc.

Schoenberg, Arnold   *Klavierstucke Op. 33a.* Belmont Music Publishers.

Schoenberg, Arnold   *Suite für Klavier Op. 25.* Belmont Music Publishers.

Scott, Cyril   *Selected Works.* G. Schirmer, Inc. [some are Intermediate]

Scriabin, Alexander   *Twenty-Four Preludes Op. 11.* Edward B. Marks Music Corp.

Shostakovitch, Dmitri   *L'Age d'Or, "Polka."* Belwin-Mills Publishing Corp.; MCA Music; G. Schirmer, Inc.; Universal Edition.

Shostakovitch, Dmitri   *24 Preludes Op. 34.* Boston Music Co.; International Music Co.; Edwin F. Kalmus; MCA Music; C. F. Peters Corp.

Shostakovitch, Dmitri   *24 Preludes and Fugues Op. 87.* Edwin F. Kalmus; MCA Music; C. F. Peters Corp.

Stevens, Halsey   *Seventeen Piano Pieces.* Editio Helios. [requires a large hand]

Szymanowski, Karol   *Mazurkas Op. 50, Book 1.* Universal Edition.

Tcherepnin, Alexander   *Bagatelles Op. 5.* Heugel et Cie.; International Music Co.; MCA Music; G. Schirmer, Inc. [some are Intermediate] Denes Agay. Yorktown Music Press. [some are Intermediate]

Webern, Anton   *Variations Op. 27 (Variationen für Klavier).* Universal Edition.

Villa-Lobos, Heitor   *The Three Maries.* Carl Fischer, Inc.

Barber, Samuel   *Nocturne.* G. Schirmer, Inc.

Copland, Aaron   *Passacaglia.* Franco Colombo Publications.

Mennin, Peter   *Five Piano Pieces.* Carl Fischer, Inc.

New Music for the Piano (Compilation of 22 Contemporary Composers), selected by Joseph Prostakoff. Lawson-Gould Music Publishers. [some are Advanced]

Palmer, Robert   *Toccata Ostinato.* Elkan-Vogel, Inc.

Prokofiev, Serge   *Four Pieces Op. 4,* "Despair." Edwin F. Kalmus; MCA Music.

Prokofiev, Serge   *Sonata No. 7.* International Music Co.; Edwin F. Kalmus; MCA Music; C. F. Peters Corp.

Prokofiev, Serge   *Suggestion Diabolique Op. 4.* Associated Music Publishers; International Music Co.; MCA Music.

Rorem, Ned   *Sonata No. 1,* "Toccata," C. F. Peters Corp.

Alfred Music Company, Inc.   75 Channel Drive, Port Washington, New York, New York 11050

Ashley Dealer's Service   263 Veteran's Blvd., Carlstadt, New Jersey 07072

Associated Music Publishers, Inc.   [see **G. Schirmer, Inc.**]

Beekman Music, Inc.   [see **Theodore Presser Company**]

Belmont Music Publishers   P.O. Box 49961, Los Angeles, California 90049

Belwin-Mills Publishing Corp.   25 Deshon Drive, Melville, New York 11746

Joseph Boonin, Inc.   P.O. Box 2124, Hackensack, New Jersey 07606

Boosey & Hawkes, Inc.   30 West 57th Street, New York, New York 10019

J & W Chester, Limited   Eagle Court, London, England EC1M 5QD [distributed by **Magnamusic-Baton, Inc.**]

Franco Colombo Publications, Inc.   [see **Belwin-Mills Publishing Corp.**]

Oliver Ditson Company   [see **Theodore Presser Company**]

Dover Publications, Inc.   180 Varick Street, New York, New York 10014

Durand et Cie.   [see **Theodore Presser Company**]

Editio Helios   Box 4012, Champaign, Illinois 61820

Editions Salabert, Inc.   575 Madison Avenue, New York, New York 10022

Elkan-Vogel, Inc.   [see **Theodore Presser Company**]

Carl Fischer, Inc.   62 Cooper Square, New York, New York 10003

J. Fischer and Bros.   [see **Belwin-Mills Publishing Corp.**]

Sam Fox Publishing Company, Inc.   P.O. Box 850, Valley Forge, Pennsylvania 19482

General Words and Music Company   [see **Neil A. Kjos Music Company**]

Henmar Press, Inc.   [see **C. F. Peters Corp.**]

Heritage Music Press   [see **Ashley Dealers Service**]

Heugel et Cie.   [see **Theodore Presser Company**]

International Music Company   509 Fifth Avenue, New York, New York 10017

Iroquois Press   London, Ontario, Canada

Edwin F. Kalmus   Miami-Dade Industrial Park, P.O. Box 1007, Opa-Locka, Florida 33054 [distributed by **Belwin-Mills Publishing Corp.**]

Neil A. Kjos Music Company   4382 Jutland Drive, San Diego, California 92117

Lawson-Gould Music Publishers, Inc.   866 Third Avenue, New York, New York 10022

Magnamusic-Baton, Inc.   10370 Page Industrial Blvd., St. Louis, Missouri 63132

Edward B. Marks Music Corp.   1790 Broadway, New York, New York 10019 [distributed by **Belwin-Mills Publishing Corp.**]

MCA Music   445 Park Avenue, New York, New York 10022 [distributed by **Belwin-Mills Publishing Corp.**]

Mercury Music, Inc.   [see **Theodore Presser Company**]
Merion Music, Inc.   [see **Theodore Presser Company**]
Myklas Press   Box 929, Boulder, Colorado 80302
Oxford University Press, Inc.   200 Madison Avenue, New York, New York 10016
C. F. Peters Corp.   373 Park Avenue South, New York, New York 10016
Theodore Presser Company   Presser Place, Bryn Mawr, Pennsylvania 19010
G. Schirmer, Inc.   866 Third Avenue, New York, New York 10022
Schmitt, Hall and McCreary Company   110 North Fifth Street, Minneapolis, Minnesota 55403
Schott and Company   [see **Belwin-Mills Publishing Corp.**]
Schroeder & Gunther   [see **G. Schirmer, Inc.**]
Shawnee Press, Inc.   Delaware Water Gap, Pennsylvania 18327
Sonos Music Resources, Inc.   Department CM, 1800 South State, Orem, Utah 84057
Southern Music Publishing Company   1619 Broadway, New York, New York 10019
Summy-Birchard Company   1834 Ridge Avenue, Evanston, Illinois 60204
Alec Templeton, Inc.   [see **Shawnee Press, Inc.**]
Universal Edition A.G.   Postfach 3, A-1015, Vienna, Austria [distributed by **Joseph Boonin, Inc.**]
Warner Bros. Publications, Inc.   75 Rockefeller Plaza, New York, New York 10019
Waterloo Music Company, Ltd.   3 Regina Street, North, Waterloo, Ontario, Canada
Yorktown Music Press   33 West 60th Street, New York, New York 10023

Index